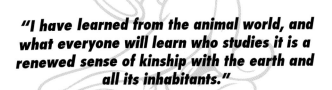

"I have learned from the animal world, and what everyone will learn who studies it is a renewed sense of kinship with the earth and all its inhabitants."

—Walt Disney, on the lessons learned through his interest in wildlife and the environment

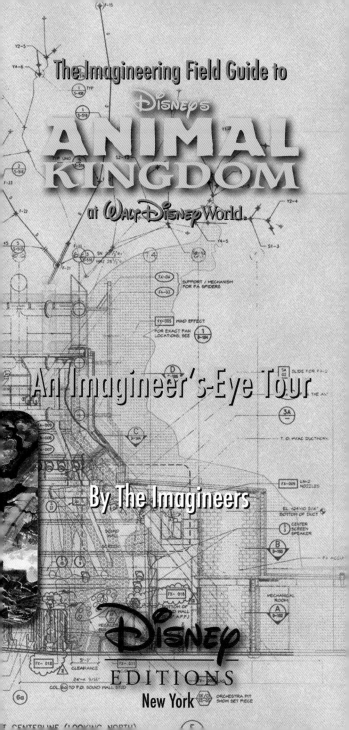

The Imagineering Field Guide to

DISNEY'S

ANIMAL KINGDOM

at Walt Disney World.

An Imagineer's-Eye Tour

By The Imagineers

DISNEY
EDITIONS
New York

For information address Disney Editions, 114 Fifth Avenue, New York, New York 10011–5690.

Printed in Malaysia

The following are some of the trademarks, registered marks, and service marks owned by Disney Enterprises, Inc.: Adventureland® Area, Audio-Animatronics®, DinoLand, U.S.A.® Area, Dinosaur Attraction, Discovery Island® Area, Disney®, Disneyland® Park, Disneyland® Resort, Disneyland® Resort Paris, Disney's Animal Kingdom® Theme Park, Disney's California Adventure® Park, *Epcot*®, Expedition Everest–Legend of the Forbidden Mountain™, Fantasyland® Area, Imagineering, Imagineers, "it's a small world," *It's Tough To Be A Bug!*® Attraction, Kali River Rapid® Attraction, Kilimanjaro Safaris® Expedition, Magic Kingdom® Park, Maharajah Jungle Trek®, Main Street, U.S.A.® Area, Pangani Forest Exploration Trail® Walking Tour, Primeval Whirl® Attraction, Tokyo Disneyland® Park, Tokyo Disneysea®, Tree of Life® Attraction, The Boneyard® Dig Site, Walt Disney World® Resort, Wildlife Express®

A Bug's Life and *Finding Nemo* characters © Disney • Pixar

Indiana Jones™ Adventure © Disney/Lucasfilm, Ltd.

For Disney Editions
Editorial Director: Wendy Lefkon
Senior Editor: Jody Revenson
Editorial Assistant: Jessica Ward

Written and Designed by Alex Wright with help from all the Imagineers

For RocketDog & Edison, the coolest animals I know

The author would like to thank Jason Surrell for his ongoing support; Scott Otis for the continued use of his extensive Disney library; Darryl Pickett for helping him get a handle on this park; Jody Revenson and Jessica Ward for their continued guidance; David Buckley for the use of his Sorcerer Mickey illustration on the cover; Gary Landrum for access to his SQS collections; Denise Brown for always being there to answer an image question; Marty Sklar and Tom Fitzgerald for their input and for letting him do another one of these; Jennifer Gerstin, Jim Clark, and Steve Cook for keeping everybody informed; Dave Smith and Robert Tieman for yet another thorough review; Cicero Greathouse, John Mazzella, and Rhonda Counts for their wonderful stories and art direction; Joe Rohde for a great park and many great opportunities; Kim, Finn, and Lincoln for giving Daddy the time to work on his book; and all Imagineers past and present for their assistance and for all the inspiration they've provided through the years.

Library of Congress Cataloging-in-Publication Data on file.

ISBN 13: 978–1-4231-0320-2
ISBN 10: 1-4231-0320-3

First Edition
10 9 8 7 6 5 4 3 2 1

TABLE OF CONTENTS

A Brief History of Imagineering

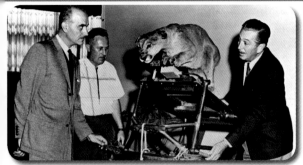

Walt Disney with a cougar from Mine Train Through Nature's Wonderland at Disneyland

The Ultimate Workshop

Walt Disney Imagineering (WDI) is the design and development arm of The Walt Disney Company. "Imagineering" is Walt Disney's combination of the words *imagination* and *engineering*, pointing out the combination of skills embodied by the group. Imagineers are responsible for designing and building Disney parks, resorts, cruise ships, and other entertainment venues. WDI is a highly creative organization, with a broad range of skills and talents represented. Disciplines range from writers to architects, artists to engineers, and cover all the bases in between. Imagineers are playful, dedicated, and abundantly curious.

Walt was our first Imagineer, but as soon as he began developing the early ideas for Disneyland, he started recruiting others to help him realize his dream. He snapped up several of his most trusted and versatile animators and art directors to apply the skills of filmmaking to the three-dimensional world. They approached this task much the same as they would a film project. They wrote stories, drew storyboards, created inspirational art, assigned the production tasks to the various film-based disciplines, and built the whole thing from scratch. Disneyland is essentially a movie that allows you to walk right in and join in the fun. As Imagineer par excellence John Hench was fond of saying in response to recent trends, "Virtual reality is nothing new . . . we've been doing that for more than fifty years!"

WDI was founded on December 16, 1952, under the name WED Enterprises (from the initials **W**alter **E**lias **D**isney). Imagineering has been an integral part of the the company's culture ever since. Imagineers are the ones who ask the "what ifs?" and "why nots?" that lead to some of our most visible and most beloved landmarks. Collectively, the Disney parks have become the physical embodiment of all that our company's mythologies represent to kids of all ages.

The Dreaming Continues

Today's Imagineering is a vast and varied group, involved in projects all over the world in every stage of development, from initial conception right through to installation and even beyond that into support and constant improvement efforts. In addition to our headquarters in Glendale, California, near the company's Burbank studios, Imagineers are based at all field locations around the world. Additionally, WDI serves as a creative resource for the entire Walt Disney Company, bringing new ideas and new technologies to all of our storytellers.

Okay, Here's the Résumé

To date, Imagineers have built eleven Disney theme parks, a town, two cruise ships, dozens of resort hotels, water parks, shopping centers, sports complexes, and various entertainment venues worldwide. Some specific highlights include:

- Disneyland (1955)
- Magic Kingdom Park (1971)
- *Epcot* ® (1982)
- Tokyo Disneyland (1983)
- Disney Studios (1989)
- Typhoon Lagoon (1989)
- Pleasure Island (1989)
- Disneyland Resort Paris (1992)
- Town of Celebration (1994)
- Blizzard Beach (1995)
- Disney's Animal Kingdom Park (1998)
- DisneyQuest (1998)
- Disney Cruise Line (*Magic,* 1998; *Wonder,* 1999)
- ABC Times Square Studios (2000)
- Disney's California Adventure Park (2001)
- Tokyo DisneySea (2001)
- Walt Disney Studios Park Paris (2002)
- Hong Kong Disneyland (2005)

He's on Our Name Tags

The red-robed Mickey Mouse with the blue hat, who is typically used to represent WDI, is taken from his Sorcerer's Apprentice character in the classic 1940 Disney film *Fantasia.* Sorcerer Mickey is symbolic of WDI's traditional position as the loyal group of magic makers at the hand of Walt Disney, the ultimate wizard. It's worth noting that the sorcerer in *Fantasia* was named Yen Sid, or the name "Disney" spelled backward.

WDI Disciplines

Imagineers form a diverse organization, with over 140 different job titles working toward the common goal of telling great stories. WDI has an exceptionally broad collection of disciplines considering its size, due to the highly specialized nature of our work. In everything it does, WDI is supported by many other divisions of The Walt Disney Company.

Harambe concept by Tom Gilleon

Show/Concept Design and Illustration produces the early drawings and renderings that serve as the inspiration for our projects, and provides the initial concepts and visual communication. This artwork gives the entire team a shared vision.

Show Writing develops the stories we want to tell in the parks, as well as any nomenclature that is required. This group writes the scripts for our attractions, the copy for plaques, and names our lands, rides, shops, vehicles, and restaurants.

Architecture is responsible for turning those fanciful show drawings into real buildings, meeting all of the functional requirements that are expected of them. Our parks present some unique architectural challenges.

Serka Zong elevation by Stefan Hellwig

Interior fixtures at Disney Outfitters

Interior Designers are responsible for the design details on the inside of our buildings. They develop the look and feel of interior spaces, and select finishes, furniture, and fixtures to complete the design.

Engineering disciplines at WDI set our mechanical, electrical, and other standards and make all of our ideas work. Engineers design structures and systems for our buildings, bridges, ride systems, and play spaces, and solve the tricky problems we throw their way every day.

Lighting Design puts all the hard work the rest of us have done on our shows and attractions into the best light. Lighting designers are also responsible for specifying all of the themed lighting fixtures found in the parks. As our lighting designers are fond of telling us, "without lights, it's radio!"

Character lighting in Creature Comforts

Marquee designed by Jason Renfroe

Graphic Designers produce signage, both flat and dimensional, in addition to providing lots of the artwork, patterns, and details that finish the Disney show. Marquees and directional signs are just a couple of examples of their work.

Prop Design is concerned with who "lives" in a given area of a park. All of the pieces and parts of everyday life that tell you about a person or a location are very carefully selected and placed. These props have to be found, purchased, prepped, built, and installed.

Propping in the Kali River Rapids queue

"Song of the Rainforest" at Conservation Station

Sound Designers work to develop the auditory backdrop for everything you see and experience. Sound is one of the most evocative senses. The songs in the attractions, the background music in the lands, and the sound effects built into show elements all work together to complete our illusions.

Media Design creates all of the various film, video, audio, and on-screen interactive content in our parks. Theme Park Productions, Inc. (TPP), a sister company to WDI, serves as something of an in-house production studio.

Screen image from It's Tough To Be A Bug!

Landscape Architecture is the discipline that focuses on our tree and plant palette and area development. This includes the layout of all of our hardscape and the arrangement of foliage elements on and between attractions.

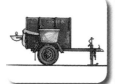

Show Set Design takes concepts and breaks them down into bite-size pieces that are organized into drawing and drafting packages, integrated into the architectural, mechanical, civil, or other components of the project, and tracked during fabrication.

Show set design by Alex Wright

Character Paint creates the reproductions of various materials, finishes, and states of aging whenever we need to make something new look old.

Character Plaster produces the hard finishes in the Park that mimic other materials. This includes rock work, themed paving, and architectural facades such as faux stone and plaster. They even use concrete to imitate wood!

Dimensional Design is the art of model making and sculpture. This skill is used to work out design issues ahead of time in model form, ensuring that our relative scales and spatial relationships are properly coordinated. Models are a wonderful tool for problem-solving.

Yeti study model by Doug Griffith

Fabrication Design involves developing and implementing the production strategies that allow us to build all the specialized items on the large and complex projects that we deliver. Somebody has to figure out how to build the impossible!

Special Effects creates all of the magical (but also totally believable) smoke, fire, lightning, ghosts, explosions, pixie dust, water, wind, rain, snow, and sparks that give our stories action and a sense of surprise. Some of these effects are quite simple, while others rely on the most sophisticated technologies that can be drawn from the field of entertainment or any other imaginable industry.

Even a waterfall is a special effect in a Disney park.

Fence detail by Alex Wright

Production Design starts with the show design, takes it to the next level of detail, and ensures that it can be built so as to maintain the creative intent. It also has the task of integrating the show with all the other systems that will need to be coordinated in the field during installation.

Master Planning looks into the future and maps out the best course of action for laying out all of our properties for development. In fact, they see further into the future than any other Imagineering division, often working with an eye toward projects that might be many years away from realization.

R&D stands for Research & Development. WDI R&D is the group that gets to play with the coolest toys. They investigate all the latest technologies from every field of study and look for ways to apply them to Disney entertainment, often inventing new ways to utilize those developments. R&D serves as a resource for the entire company.

Project Management is responsible for organizing our teams, schedules, and processes so that our projects can be delivered when they're supposed to be, within a financial framework and at the expected level of quality.

Construction Management ensures that every job meets the Disney construction standards, including quality control, code compliance, and long-term durability during operation.

Imagineering Lingo

WDI has a very vibrant and unique culture, which is even embodied in the terms we throw around the office when we're working. Here is a guide to help you understand us a bit better as we show you around the Park.

Area Development - The interstitial spaces between the attractions, restaurants, and shops. This would include landscape architecture, propping, show elements, and special enhancements intended to expand the experience.

Audio-Animatronics - The term for the three-dimensional animated human and animal characters we employ to perform in our shows and attractions. Audio-Animatronics was invented by Imagineers at Walt's request and is an essential component of many iconic Disney attractions.

Berm - A raised earthen barrier, typically heavily landscaped, which serves to eliminate visual intrusions into the Park from the outside world and block the outside world from intruding inside.

BGM - Background Music. The musical selections that fill in the audio landscape as you make your way around the Park. Each BGM track is carefully selected, arranged, and recorded to enhance the story being told.

Blue Sky - The early stages in the idea-generation process when anything is possible. There are not yet any considerations taken into account that might rein in the creative process. At this point, the sky's the limit!

Brainstorm - A gathering for the purpose of generating as many ideas as possible in the shortest time possible. We hold many brainstorming sessions at WDI, always looking for the best ideas. Imagineering has a set of Brainstorming Rules, which are always adhered to.

> **Rule 1** - There is no such thing as a bad idea. We never know how one idea (however far-fetched) might lead into another one that is exactly right.
>
> **Rule 2** - We don't talk yet about *why not*. There will be plenty of time for realities later, so we don't want them to get in the way of the good ideas now.
>
> **Rule 3** - Nothing should stifle the flow of ideas. No buts or can'ts or other "stopping" words. We want to hear words such as "and," "or," and "what if?"
>
> **Rule 4** - There is no such thing as a bad idea. (We take that one very seriously.)

Charrette - Another term for a brainstorming session. From the French word for "cart." It refers to the cart sent through the Latin Quarter in Paris to collect the art and design projects of students at the legendary École des Beaux-Arts who were unable to deliver them to the school themselves after the mad rush to complete their work at the end of the term.

Concept - An idea and the effort put into communicating it and developing it into something usable. A concept can be expressed as a drawing, a written description, or simply a verbal pitch. Everything we do starts out as a concept.

Dark Ride - A term often used to describe the charming little Fantasyland attractions housed more or less completely inside a show building, which allows for greater isolation of show elements and light control, as needed.

Elevation - A drawing of a true frontal view of an object—usually a building—often drawn from multiple sides, eliminating the perspective that you would see in the real world, for clarity in the design and to lead construction activities.

E-Ticket - The top level of attractions. This dates back to an early Disneyland ticketing system used to distribute ridership through all attractions in the Park. Each was assigned a letter (A,B,C,D,E) indicating where it fell in the Park's pecking order.

Kinetics – Movement and motion in a scene that give it life and energy. This can come from moving vehicles, active signage, changes in the lighting, special effects, or even hanging banners or flags that move around as the wind blows.

Maquette – A model, especially a sculpture, depicting a show element in miniature scale so that design issues can be worked out before construction begins. It's much easier to make changes on a maquette than on a full-size anything.

Plan – A direct overhead view of an object or a space. Very useful in verifying relative sizes of elements and the flow of Guests and show elements through an area.

Plussing – A word derived from Walt's penchant for always trying to make an idea better. Imagineers are continually trying to *plus* their work, even after it's "finished."

POV – Point Of View. The position from which something is seen, or the place an artist chooses to use as the vantage point of the imaginary viewer in a concept illustration. POVs are chosen in order to best represent the idea being shown.

Propping – The placement of objects around a scene. From books on a shelf to place settings on a table to wall hangings in an office space, props are the elements that give a set life and describe the people who live there. They are the everyday objects we see all around but that point out so much about us if you pay attention to them.

Section – A drawing that looks as if it's a slice through an object or space. This is very helpful in seeing how various elements interrelate. It is typically drawn as though it were an elevation, with heavier line weights defining where our imaginary cut would be.

Show – Everything we put "onstage" in a Disney park. Walt believed that everything we put out for the Guests in our parks was part of a big show, so much of our terminology originated in the show business world. With that in mind, *show* becomes for us a very broad term that includes just about anything our Guests see, hear, smell, or come in contact with during their visit to any of our parks or resorts.

Story – Story is the fundamental building block of everything WDI does. Imagineers are, above all, storytellers. The time, place, characters, and plot points that give our work meaning start with the story, which is also the framework that guides all design decisions.

Storyboard – A large pin-up board used to post ideas in a charrette or to outline the story points of a ride or film. The technique was perfected by Walt in the early days of his animation studio and became a staple of the animated film development process. The practice naturally transferred over to WDI when so many of the early Imagineers came over from Walt's Animation department.

Theme – The fundamental nature of a story in terms of what it means to us, or the choice of time, place, and decor applied to an area in order to support that story.

THRC – Theoretical Hourly Ride Capacity. The number of guests per hour that can experience an attraction under optimal conditions. THRC is always taken into account when a new attraction is under consideration.

Visual Intrusion – Any outside element that makes its way into a scene, breaks the visual continuity, and destroys the illusion. WDI works hard to eliminate visual intrusions.

Wienie – Walt's playful term for a visual element that could be used to draw people into and around a space. A wienie is big enough to be seen from a distance and interesting enough to make you want to take a closer look, like the Tree of Life, or Expedition Everest viewed across Discovery Lake. Wienies are critical to our efforts at laying out a sequence of experiences in an organized fashion.

DISNEY'S ANIMAL KINGDOM

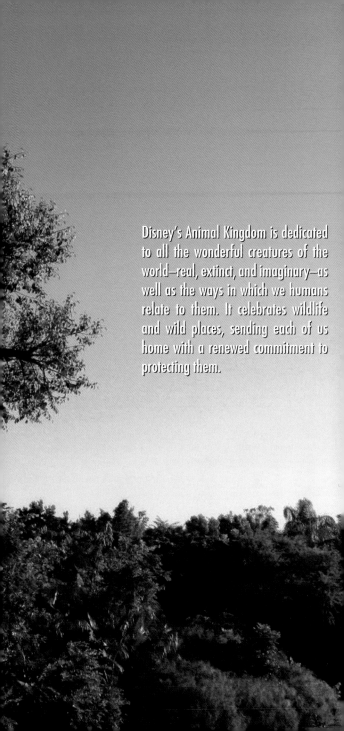

Disney's Animal Kingdom is dedicated to all the wonderful creatures of the world—real, extinct, and imaginary—as well as the ways in which we humans relate to them. It celebrates wildlife and wild places, sending each of us home with a renewed commitment to protecting them.

Animal Instincts

Walt Disney in his office with a couple of friends

The Walt Disney Company has always had a tremendous association with animals. This long-standing connection is derived in large part from the studio's animated cartoons. Walt always felt that animals offered tremendous character studies. Animals offer a variety of personalities, either real or imagined, and provide story settings far broader than that of humans. So a vast number of characters in the Disney canon are of animal origin, as lead characters and supporting cast.

When Walt and his team went about developing the animal characters for his animated films, he insisted that the animators learn as much as possible about their subjects. The artists were required to read about the particular animal they were designing, go to see them at the zoo if possible, and even attend life-drawing classes at the studio, drawing the animal from a real-life example brought in by Walt. By understanding the animals' physiology, the artists could better illustrate their movements in their drawings, however stylized the designs might be. A greater degree of naturalism could be built into the character's actions by learning about their habits and tendencies, offering story and gag possibilities while maintaining the believability of the character.

Walt pursued his interest in animals on other fronts, as well. His True-Life Adventures series was launched with the release of *Seal Island* in 1948. This was the first of thirteen nature films produced by the studio through 1960. Eight of these films won Academy Awards. His approach with these nature films was equally character driven, telling stories assembled in the editing room from the miles and miles of footage brought back by the film crews. These films succeeded, and even thrived, at a time when distributors were skeptical that audiences would be willing to sit through a half-hour-long nature documentary.

During the production of Bambi in the early 1940s, Walt had live deer brought into the studio so that his animators could capture the movement and behavior of the deer and other woodland creatures.

This would become standard practice over the years. Dogs were brought in for Lady and the Tramp, baby elephants for Dumbo, and big cats for The Lion King. For Tarzan, however, the animators went to a local zoo near the studio to observe gorillas.

All in Good Time

It was always Walt's intention to have live animals in a Disney park. His original plan for Jungle Cruise at Disneyland called for real animals to be featured along the shores of the rivers of the world. At the time, the logistics involved didn't allow for it, and the reality was that the animals wouldn't have allowed for the consistent show Walt wanted to provide for his audience. This dilemma did, however, lead to the development of the animated figures that populate the banks of Jungle Cruise and eventually to the wonderful birds of The Enchanted Tiki Room—our first Audio-Animatronics attraction, which debuted in 1963. The more naturalistic story lines of Animal Kingdom are a better fit for live animals than the more theatrical approach of Disneyland.

Walt admiring the stars of The Enchanted Tiki Room at Disneyland

Bird's-eye view of the Park by Dan Goozee

A New Challenge for Imagineering

During construction, a license plate seen frequently on the front car bumpers of the Imagineers who worked on the site for Disney's Animal Kingdom read, "A New Species of Theme Park." There was a great deal of truth to that sentiment. Animal Kingdom is perhaps the most distinct Disney park, with a *nature* decidedly its own and quite unique in all the world. This new park, dedicated to the spirit of wildlife and wild places, required an entirely different design approach than the methods the Imagineers had honed over forty years since the design and construction of the original Disneyland Park.

Certainly the same tools were brought to bear on the task—the usual scenic devices, all of our varied production skills, and the carefully developed visual storytelling—but the goals of the effort were quite new to us. In contrast to our typical assignments to create fully realized visions of fantastical environments, or heightened realities that never really existed except in our collective memories, this time we had to create entirely real places. Real places that *felt* like real places. Real places as they exist in the real world right now. The introduction of live animals into a park environment trumped any other design element. There is nothing more real than these animals—they eat, sleep, hide, sleep, eat, and sleep some more (largely beyond our control). This reality permeated every facet of our design process, from the earliest gathering of reference material to the in-depth research to the in-field art direction and execution of the concept. The need to match the reality of the animals became a rallying cry for those involved in carrying it out and gives the Park its unique identity in the world of Disney theme parks.

A Park with a Life of Its Own

Animal Kingdom was designed to grow, develop, and evolve over time, even beyond the normal caretaking and plussing from the Imagineers. We never believe that our parks are complete at Opening Day, but the changes expected at Animal Kingdom went beyond the normal additions and alterations that come with time. Many elements of this park were never expected to remain in their current state.

The tree canopy over Discovery Island, for example, is envisioned as one day rising entirely above the roofs of the buildings, making the architecture even more subservient to the natural environment. This will also alter the relationship between the Tree of Life—which, as real as it may appear, won't continue to grow—and the rest of the surrounding natural foliage.

The landscape design of this Park also differs from the others, in that the goal is not to create a timeless, unchanging image that will be consistent from day to day and year to year. At Animal Kingdom, the plants are intended to grow, blossom, die, and rot in a cyclical system that will be different each time a Guest comes to visit. While the Park's horticulture staff works hard to maintain the plant life, they work under a different set of marching orders than the staffs at other Disney parks.

The waterways of Animal Kingdom—Discovery River and Discovery Lake— are living, breathing ecosystems with lives of their own. They have native plants, Florida wildlife, and will certainly grow their own way over time.

Clearly the animals bring another type of life cycle to the Park. They are born here, they grow, they age, and eventually they die. This "Circle of Life" serves as the conceptual underpinning of all of the stories we tell at Animal Kingdom.

Early concept for Park entrance by Joe Rohde

Park entrance concept by Gerry Dunn

Not (Just) a Zoo

Disney's Animal Kingdom is an accredited zoo, but it's also much more than that. It is a theme park featuring stories about animals and the ways in which humans interact with them. As such, it is capable of delving into levels of intellectual stimulation that are beyond the reach of zoos that merely present animals to view and offer accompanying information to round out the experience. Those facilities typically don't have at their disposal the resources or the storytelling background to go any further. Animal Kingdom is built on a story foundation that encompasses three major realms of how we interact with animals. These three categories establish the progression that one experiences in a day at the Park. It is a very carefully established relationship that was central to the Park's early development.

First, there are areas of the Park that focus on elevating appreciation of animals and awareness of the issues relating to them. We share the world with real animals. They are seen in zoos, on television, in film, and in books. They are impacted by our actions every day. It is important that we learn about these animals so that any negative impacts we have on them or their ecosystems might be lessened, and so that we can work toward a harmonic balance between us, the wildlife, and the environment. These animals drive the action in Oasis, Africa, Asia, and Rafiki's Planet Watch.

Secondly, the Park contains references to extinct animals. We see them either through reconstructions of their fossils or artistic representations of their likenesses. We see these animals in books or on television and, certainly, in the movies. Man has a deep-rooted fascination with them that seems to transcend time. This is the primary focus of Dinoland, USA.

The last story category is that of mythical animals and the various forms that they take. In truth, this group says more about humans than it does about animals—for it has to do with the attributes that we project onto animals. We assign them personality characteristics for use in our stories, such as referring to a lion, Simba, as the king of the animals, or holding a belief that a Yeti assumes the responsibility of protecting a mountain. This concept will continue to be developed over time.

The progression through the Park also leads us through a planned series of adventures. The cumulative effect of these experiences is intended to lead to an end result that can have real value in the real world.

- We begin by being enthralled by the beauty of nature in the Oasis. This leads us away from our everyday world and prepares us for what's to come.

- We see a whimsical representation of our abiding love for animals in Discovery Island. Here we are reminded of the bounty and diversity to be found in the animal world.

- Camp Minnie-Mickey is an introduction to animals as story time friends, which for many of us was one of our earliest connections to the concept of animals.

- Dinoland, USA shows us how human curiosity can and does lead to discoveries about animals, and, in effect, bring them to life.

- Africa and Asia offer the most realistic look at the boundary between the human and animal worlds today, and point out the necessity of good environmental decision-making as that boundary is redefined over time.

- Rafiki's Planet Watch invites us to take the next step—becoming personally involved. It shows us how to take this inspiration home with us, and offers ideas for making a real difference in our own neighborhoods or anywhere in the world.

Oasis carousel concept by Joe Rohde

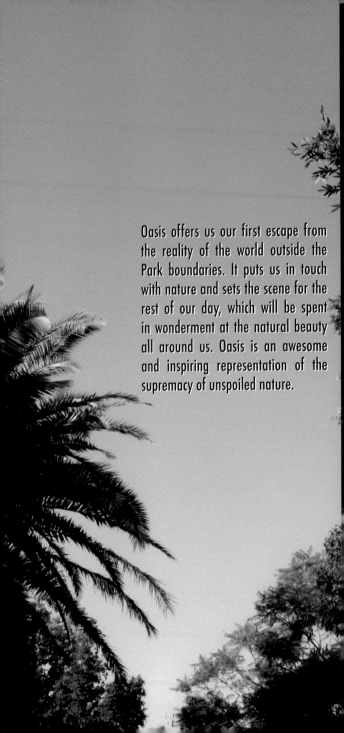

Oasis offers us our first escape from the reality of the world outside the Park boundaries. It puts us in touch with nature and sets the scene for the rest of our day, which will be spent in wonderment at the natural beauty all around us. Oasis is an awesome and inspiring representation of the supremacy of unspoiled nature.

Overlook in Genesis Gardens by Bryan Jowers

A Natural Progression

Oasis serves much the same function here as Main Street, U.S.A., does at Magic Kingdom Park. It creates a dramatic break from the world outside and takes us back to a simpler time. In this case, back to the realm of unspoiled nature—to a time when the complex issues addressed in the rest of the Park have not yet arisen. It sets up the comparisons and contrasts to the world we know that are so central to our stories.

Oasis separates the Park from the outside world by creating a buffer zone for those entering through the gates. The architectural style of the entry complex—based on that of the American Arts and Crafts architecture prevalent in Southern California in the early 20th century—is very carefully chosen so as to be secondary to the surrounding environment. Craftsman architecture is known for making extensive use of natural elements in its surface treatments, as well as for the application of a very hand-hewn aesthetic regarding the carpentry and masonry. This sense of texture suggests to the observer a relationship between the built and the natural environment that is harmonious and interwoven. This design and construction approach is very much in keeping with the underlying spirit of the Park.

Oasis gateways with the Tree of Life in the background, illustrated by Dave Minichiello

Allow Me to Introduce You...

We approach Oasis from our worldly realm across an expanse of parking lot that is very familiar to us in our day-to-day lives. But as we enter, the paving on the promenade becomes more naturalistic, with a pitted texture and a mottled color palette. Embedded in the promenade is a subtle pattern featuring a graphic representation of the Tree of Life.

The Park entry complex introduces the stories of the Park through the animal sculptures rendered over the arbor and transitions us to the winding pathways and dense vegetation of the Oasis gardens. Here we find peaceful settings, fascinating animals in close proximity, rushing waterfalls, and a variety of plants drawn from the most lush and exotic locales on the planet. The sense of kinship with our fellow inhabitants of this world, which is established by this place, will affect our perception of the various settings and experiences to be found throughout the rest of the Park. It's a form of nostalgia not unlike the sense we get walking down Main Street with its turn-of-the-century atmosphere—comforting us and reminding us of simpler times.

Does This Look Familiar to You?

We exit Oasis via a pair of rockwork portals that are reminiscent of the forms of the train station at the Magic Kingdom. We come around a corner, pass through the archways to the bridge, and are presented with our first view of the Tree of Life—in much the same manner as the first time we see Cinderella Castle. Over the course of this journey, we have made our way from the elevation of the parking lot—roughly that of the original Park site prior to construction—slowly but surely up to an elevation nearly twenty feet higher. By entering Discovery Island at that elevation, we are ensured of a clear vista, over the heads of fellow Guests up ahead, and we are able to see the Tree of Life in all of its glory—without allowing it to tower completely above us.

The Unstructured Theme Park

Animal Kingdom vs. Disneyland

There are several ways in which the design approach to Disney's Animal Kingdom differs from that of our other parks. For more than fifty years, Disneyland has been our reference point and the model for most of the structural elements of a new park, such as park icons, entry points, circulation routes, and progression through story lines. Animal Kingdom certainly takes lessons from Disneyland, but the design team chose to tweak some of those elements for very specific reasons.

Much of the variation can be seen when we compare Oasis to Main Street, U.S.A., at Disneyland—and our other Magic Kingdom parks around the world—or to Hollywood Boulevard at the Disney Studios, or even the entry plaza in front of Spaceship Earth at Epcot. Oasis clearly serves the same function, but does so in strikingly different ways. These differences are instrumental in explaining to our Guests how a day at Animal Kingdom will differ from a day at one of the other parks.

A Disney park typically greets the Guest at the entrance with an architectural face—often a large, fairly urban design aesthetic using some fanciful architectural statement that exemplifies the theme of the park. At Animal Kingdom, we tell a story that is dominated by nature, so the primary statement at our entry is the abrupt change between the hard, formal surfaces of the entry plaza and the near lack of human influence experienced in Oasis. Even the requisite manufactured elements of this land are designed to be minimally intrusive into the natural environment. The handrails are hand wrought from natural materials, as are the animal identification graphics. These are also placed very low in one's field of view so that they are less invasive.

The landscape design of the Park in many cases takes the place of the formal elements we often employ. Here in Oasis, the architecture is formed by the foliage. Just past the turnstiles, we encounter two stands of *Phoenix reclinata*, reflective of a formal gateway. Once in Oasis, the various animal habitats are "rooms" forming something akin to the storefronts on Main Street, U.S.A.

Animal Kingdom is also about discovery, and the reward that comes with exploration. Instead of a long corridor directing us straight toward a large park icon, or "wienie," we are immediately presented with two pathways, each offering a different reward. It is up to us, as the Guest, to determine our path. If we venture down some of the side paths, we find still other rewards, such as additional animal habitats or a suspension bridge through a waterfall.

Design detail for the sloth habitat by TA Strawser

It Only *Looks* Like It's Been There for Thousands of Years

This completely designed and built space is given the responsibility of representing pure and untouched nature. The primary intent of Oasis is to make our Guests feel welcome in this world and this is the moment when the Park first puts us in touch with the wildlife and wild places that are our focus. There is an implicit conservation message imparted here, as stated in one of the project's guiding purpose statements: "You will only save what you love, and you will only love what you know."

The animals found along the path are not supposed to be "on display" so much as going about their business. It is less important for a Guest to walk up to a habitat and view an animal than for the overall perception of Oasis to be calming, soothing, and invigorating. We are here to share space with them, and get to know them.

QUICK TAKES

• Disney's Animal Kingdom has 1,500 specimens of mammals, birds, reptiles, and amphibians—representing more than 300 species—in addition to 5,000 specimens of fish comprising 50 different species and thousands of insects from over 40 different species.

• It takes about four and a half tons of food a day to keep the Park's animals happy. The Animal Nutrition Center prepares over 400 individual or group diets daily.

• The animals inhabiting Oasis were chosen because they are perceived to have a gentle disposition. This helps to achieve the sense of welcome that the land is intended to embody.

Animal Acquisition

It Takes a Village to Raise an Animal

The zoological community is one that relies greatly upon the cooperation of its various members. Facilities are constantly sharing information regarding research and the best practices for animal care. Zoologists attend conferences, present papers, and network so as to pass along any new techniques. They also move animals around from site to site in order to maintain breeding programs.

Disney's Animal Kingdom is an active participant in that community. The Animal Programs and Animal Care staffs were recruited from zoos and zoological facilities around the country, so they are very well connected. They share their findings regarding facility design, animal husbandry, and animal enrichment. Participation in industry organizations such as the American Zoo and Aquarium Association (AZA) is critical to this mission.

Sable Antelope

Once the team—the Imagineers working with Park Operations, Animal Programs, veterinary staff, the DAK Advisory Council, and any other group with a stake in the matter—determined the animal population of the Park, they had to go about procuring them. The choices made revolved around several factors such as the number of animals, number of species, size of groups in habitats, species that could be housed in mixed-species habitats, etc. Then it fell to the acquisitions group to locate available specimens.

Practically all the animals came from existing facilities, some nearby and others around the world. Some animals were purchased, others were acquired to relieve excess populations, and some were accepted on loan in order to participate in the AZA's Species Survival Program, which maintains registries to ensure the viability and genetic diversity of captive animal populations worldwide.

A hippo surfaces in the reserve.

An early resident checks out his new home.

The Long Way Home

The shortest distance between two points may be a straight line, but that doesn't mean that that was the path taken as our animals made their way from their previous homes to Disney's Animal Kingdom. Because of issues involving quarantine requirements, construction schedules, plant growth cycles, and other factors, many of the animals had to make stops along the way while waiting for their habitats to be completed.

The Animal Programs department made agreements with several facilities around the state and the country to provide temporary housing for our animals. This allowed them to serve out their quarantines, get used to new neighbors, acclimate to the weather in this area, or simply wait until their facilities were ready for them.

For example, the bat population that now lives in Maharajah Jungle Trek—along with many other of our species on their way to the Park—spent several months at the Lubee Foundation in Gainesville, Florida. This facility, one of the preeminent bat research facilities in the world, was uniquely qualified to host them, and offered the additional benefit of being located relatively close to the Animal Kingdom site. This allowed Imagineers to take field trips to see them—as a team-building exercise, to get a break from the stresses of a hectic project site, and to meet and to learn more about these fascinating creatures for whom they were building new homes.

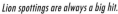
Lion spottings are always a big hit.

DISCOVERY ISLAND

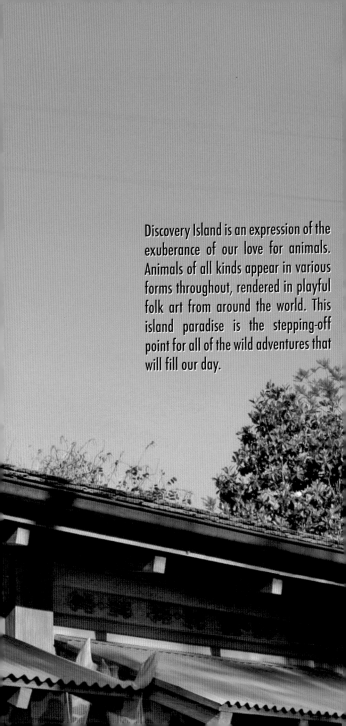

Discovery Island is an expression of the exuberance of our love for animals. Animals of all kinds appear in various forms throughout, rendered in playful folk art from around the world. This island paradise is the stepping-off point for all of the wild adventures that will fill our day.

Early Discovery Island concept by Gerry Dunn and Joe Rohde

Main Street, E.A.R.T.H.

When we design a place for a Disney park—especially a new place that doesn't truly exist in the real world—the primary driver of our design choices is the answer to the question of who "lives" there. This defines for us the architectural forms, the building materials, the types of vehicles, the propping, and any other aspect of the environment that we're going to place here. It's probably the single most important element of our story.

When Michael Eisner was considering possible names for this new park, he said, "We have the Magic Kingdom, so we should have the Animal Kingdom, too." Even then he made the point that animals could be magical—that the words were almost interchangeable in this context. Nowhere in the Park is that more evident than in Discovery Island, where its villagers and visitors alike are enchanted by the magic of animals.

The residents of Discovery Island all share an abiding love of animals—so much so that they are practically unable to contain themselves in their expression of this fascination. It finds its way out in everything the villagers produce—animals are seen on every building facade, sign, lamp, wall, and fountain in this land.

Safari Village elevation by Gerry Dunn

Discovering the Islands

Discovery Island is not based on any single place in the world, but rather an amalgamation of many places. Generally speaking, its style is based on the architecture and especially the folk art of cultures found on equatorial islands around the world—places such as Bali, the Caribbean, the South Seas Islands, and those along the coast of Africa. The architecture of Discovery Island is clean, bright, colorful, and essentially pristine. It has reached a state of harmony that removes it from the ongoing effort of standing up to the forces of nature that we see imposed on other buildings throughout the rest of the Park.

Early Discovery Island concept by Dan Sauerbrary

Island Style

Using this island folk art, the architecture of Discovery Island is designed to mirror the ideas expressed on the Tree of Life. The Tree is the natural expression of the love of animals, and the architecture is the human expression. Artwork here is integrated into the buildings in ways that are always organic to the architecture. The animal motifs are not just applied to surfaces as ornament—they are a core part of the building's design. The animal motifs always fit into a window shutter frame or run the length of a column support or form the brackets supporting the roof structure. Even the painted patterns tend to fill the surfaces onto which they are applied. Nothing is ever random or haphazard.

Building heights are restricted in the interest of maintaining the all-important balance between the landscaping and the architecture. Where it is not possible to avoid exceeding the desired building height, we employ masking and screening via partition walls or foliage to ensure that the *apparent* height of the building is within the desired range.

Some of that foliage is planted backstage, to imply that the world of Discovery Island extends beyond the land's boundary, and to offer us better planting positions for masking visual intrusions. One piece of foliage employed to this effect is a stand of bamboo behind Pizzafari that derives from one originally planted by Imagineer Bill Evans at Disneyland in 1955. A cutting was transplanted to the Magic Kingdom in 1971—also under Bill's direction—and eventually a section was moved to Animal Kingdom during construction.

Inspirational concept of the Tree of Life by Dan Goozee

I Think That I Shall Never See, a Tree as Lovely as This Tree

The Tree of Life is one of the most amazing pieces of art ever created by WDI. It's beautiful and meaningful, and captures the essence of this park at a glance. It's a poetic statement of the majesty of nature, the stunning diversity of animals, and our respect for our place in the world, and underscores the ideal that all of these elements can co-exist harmoniously. In our story, the animals are not carved into the surface—they've grown out from it. As one approaches the Tree and the animal forms begin to reveal themselves, it becomes clear that there is almost no tree at all. That tree *is* the animal kingdom.

The Tree of Life is a metaphor that exists in the mythologies of many cultures around the world. It is seen as a source of life and an emblem of symbiosis. Within the WDI mythology for Discovery Island, the Tree is supposed to have been the first thing here—the village came here to the Tree. It is the source of life and of water for the village and Discovery Island, and presumably for the rest of Animal Kingdom as well.

Does That Look Like...?

The experience of viewing the Tree of Life can be likened to that of looking for animals in the clouds. The longer one looks, the more one sees—maybe even all 325 of them. This effect is the result of very careful planning during the design phase. The development of the look of the Tree of Life was initially accomplished through numerous concept drawings and paintings, and then through an exhaustive model-making phase. The team carved renditions of the Tree in foam—first small-scale, then much larger—and then tested various paint and artificial foliage treatments on the model. This detailed process is what allowed the team in the field to maintain continuity when working at real size, as they were unable to step back and see the Tree as a whole during construction due to the scaffolding that was covering most of the surface.

Elevation of the Tree of Life by Dave Minichiello

QUICK TAKES

- The final look of the Tree of Life was based on a particular bonsai tree the design team found at the International Flower & Garden Festival at Epcot on one of their trips to Florida.

- Early plans called for Guests to be able to ascend to the top of the Tree for an overlook of Discovery Island and the rest of the Park.

- The Tree of Life serves as the icon of the Park and a wienie just like the castles at Disneyland and Magic Kingdom Park, Spaceship Earth at Epcot, and Grizzly Peak at Disney's California Adventure.

- Another early concept—The Roots Restaurant, which was to be located under the base of the Tree—was to have been the Park's finest eatery.

Early concept of a view toward the Tree of Life by Ben Tripp

Tree's Company!

Not only is the Tree of Life one of the greatest artistic feats we've ever pulled off, it's also one of the greatest engineering challenges we've taken on. The Tree of Life is a massive structure, reaching 145 feet into the air with a full canopy of natural-looking leaves, and enclosing a 420-seat theater. It has to meet the requirements for all buildings erected on property—including a 145-mph wind-load requirement.

This challenge seemed quite daunting, and the team explored numerous options for the central structure, the branch assemblies, and the leaf canopy. It didn't help that the functional requirements of this unusual building seemed to be a moving target. In fact, it was roughly halfway through the project before it was even determined that a theater would be placed inside! At one point, the primary form of the tree canopy itself was to be constructed as a geodesic dome, onto which the leaves would be applied as a surface element. This was an attempt to simplify the structural design. In the end, however, it was discovered that by the time we had engineered the structure to support the dome, we could basically support any kind of branches we wanted!

Tree of Life schematic showing geodesic canopy by Gerry Dunn

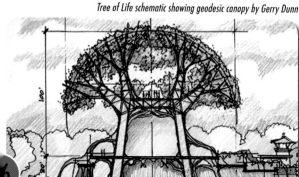

Sometimes It's Productive to Watch TV!

The real structural design breakthrough didn't come until one of the team members was watching an educational program on television that dealt with offshore oil-drilling platforms and saw an opportunity. The core structure of those platforms was just the right shape to serve as an armature for the Tree's trunk, and was certainly strong enough to support the immense loads. Once this conundrum was resolved, the rest of the plan fell into place in relatively short order.

Composite of various Tree of Life drawing packages— structural, mechanical, and architectural

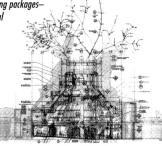

It's Not Like These Things Grow on Trees!

Even once you've decided on how you intend to go about building a tree like this, there's still a great deal of artistry required at every step of the way in order to achieve the desired result. Each layer had to be applied with a careful eye toward matching the proportions that had been so carefully laid out during the development of the design and the fabrication of the model. If any of the relationships were altered, the tree might not carry the same visual—and therefore emotional—impact when completed.

The branches were built from a diminishing-diameter series of steel pipes, with the joints angled and articulated to provide the organic forms. Onto this was applied a structural foam layer, to rough in the sculpture while minimizing the weight. This foam was coated with concrete that was embedded with a steel cage mesh. Then a team of eight Imagineering sculptors led by Character Plaster Production Designer (and resident Artist-in-Cement) Zsolt Hormay applied the final layer of plaster—two to four inches in thickness—that would serve as their artistic medium. Each sculptor was able to carve roughly a six or eight foot square area each day, approximately one medium-sized animal each. Some of the feature animals required more time to develop, occasionally with a team of two or three artists working for several days. Last came the paint treatment— our Character Paint department followed the carvers down the tree, with layers of scaffolding being removed one at a time. The entire process took just over two years, with the visible surface efforts taking up the better part of the final twelve months.

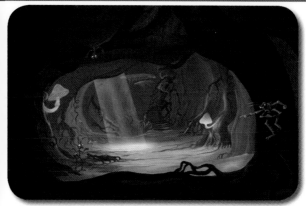

It's Tough To Be A Bug! *proscenium and show concept by Ruben Viramontes*

It's Tough To Be An Imagineer!

The stakes are very high any time we work on an attraction that is to go into one of our park icons. Such an attraction carries with it the weight of defining the park's concept, or at least to justify its placement in such a high-profile location! Spaceship Earth at Epcot describes the history of human communications, the foundation upon which all the rest of the concepts within the Park are built. At the Disney Studios park, The Great Movie Ride offers a survey of some of the most memorable moments in film history, and serves as a backdrop for the homage to movie magic represented by the rest of the Park.

For the show within the Tree of Life, the Imagineers struggled long and hard to come up with a worthy tenant. There were concepts for films and Audio-Animatronics shows, and several combinations thereof. The subject matter varied in style and tone, from majestic tributes to the wonder of nature, to character-driven fables starring the cast of the Disney animated film, *The Lion King*. All that was certain was that the show needed to carry a meaningful environmental message.

Through all of this effort, however, none of the show concepts had really gelled. Either the story didn't feel right or the setting didn't feel right to the team as they produced their storyboards and made their presentations. Finally they hit upon a concept that worked on all fronts. The upcoming Disney•Pixar film *A Bug's Life* offered a great collection of characters capable of comedy, drama, and the dissemination of information. The fact that the theater was essentially underground was actually an asset for this show, and it allowed us to tell the important story of bugs, which had proven to be difficult to work into other areas of the Park.

Thinking on Your Feet...All Six of Them

The idea for *It's Tough To Be A Bug!* came from Michael Eisner during a presentation of one of those previous concepts—a presentation that was not going well at all. The team was struggling with finding a suitable tenant for this subterranean theater. He pointed out that bugs live in (and under) trees, and that we had this great movie about bugs coming along the following year. He suggested that we go talk to Pixar Animation Studios to find out more about *A Bug's Life*, and the rest is...comedy.

These two concepts, at left by Bryan Jowers for a "wonders of nature" show, and below by Dave Minichiello for a Lion King character show, demonstrate just how broad the range of ideas considered by the Imagineers was for this very important theater.

The finished piece may be quite far-removed from the development work. While in the end it's easy to look at the concept that won out and say, "Well, of course it couldn't be any other way," it's not always so obvious at the outset.

The brainstorm paid off and then some, as the last-minute show—which went into development after the Tree of Life was already under construction—became one of the most popular of WDI's multimedia 3-D film attractions, and went on to see a subsequent installation at Disney's California Adventure Park in 2001.

Poster concepts for the Tree of Life Repertory Theater by Nicole Armitage Doolittle and Noji Milton

Integration of architecture and landscaping at Pizzafari

Nature vs. Architecture

The planning of Animal Kingdom was based around the relationship between the architectural elements—references to the influence of Man—and the natural environments into which they are placed. This relationship is instrumental to the Park's story lines. Architecture influences nature, and nature influences architecture. At no point inside the Park, however, is the architecture allowed to overwhelm the natural elements. If anything, the converse is true.

For example, the parking lot is allowed to remain relatively barren. We don't even see one of the greenbelt bands that typically break up the expanse of our theme-park lots. This contrasts with the massive berms that are visible as one approaches the Park's entrance, and ensures that the immersion into nature within Oasis will be very impactful. Discovery Island was conceived as a place in which the human inhabitants are very much in tune with nature, so the spaces are designed as a truly interconnected whole, in which Man and Nature are balanced in harmony. In Asia, buildings and statuary have been overrun by trees, establishing the preeminence of nature. We see places in which Man has allowed this relationship to slip into a state of imbalance, such as in the burn zone at the top of the mountain on Kali River Rapids. Through most of the Park, nature remains most prominent, with height limitations on the buildings and a landscape design scheme that establishes this relationship.

This leads to a very different approach to the maintenance of the Park's landscape design as it ages and evolves. The expectation is that the foliage will grow and reshape itself, in a way that's not allowed in our other parks, and eventually achieve a new relationship of scale compared to the built environment.

Theme vs. Setting

The design approach to Animal Kingdom, from its outset, has been an unusually literary one. Even the word "theme" can take on a different meaning for the Animal Kingdom team. Here, when we use the term, we are more interested in what something *means* than what it *looks like*. We build park elements around core themes that have served as the foundations of story and formed the basis of mythologies throughout human history. It is these themes that drive every one of our design decisions throughout the development process.

"Theme" is a noun rather than a verb. It is sometimes mistakenly taken to mean applying ornament to an object to make it appear to belong to a particular time or place, such as the architecture or propping found in Main Street, U.S.A., Frontierland, or Fantasyland. Those details, however, really only relate to a setting.

Consider this design exercise relating to the design of a familiar setting. We could choose to tell any sort of a story in "The Old West," where Frontierland at Magic Kingdom Park is set, but the story that we choose to tell will have a tremendous impact on what that place will look like. For a gritty story of great conflict, we might tend toward angular and asymmetrical building silhouettes, roughly-textured materials, and heavily weathered surfaces. For the Frontierland story, however—a tale of great optimism—we choose to create warm, comfortable, inviting spaces with facades rendered in rustic materials and a general sense of order throughout. Without that structure, we have nothing to drive your decisions, and they become random. If you were to design a space in which to tell a story without knowing what the story was going to be, you might end up with an entirely incongruous collection of images.

The design team spends a significant amount of time studying the thematic basis of any element being considered for the Park before ever picking up a pencil to draw. The Animal Kingdom team is hesitant to move quickly into the drawing and illustration phase, for fear of getting too far along the wrong design path before resolving entirely what we want to say with a new project. The design images that WDI creates can be very persuasive and can sometimes get people excited about what it is that's being conceived, even if it's really just in its earliest stages. People have strong attachments to images and can have difficulty considering other possibilities once they have gotten their minds set on one. Executive Designer Joe Rohde has referred to this as the "kitten-in-a-box" syndrome, by which you can't get away from that first image because everyone who sees it falls in love with it.

Tree of Life Gardens

Two topis butting heads along the trail of the Tree of Life Gardens

Off the Beaten Path

In another of the smaller-scale side trips offered to Guests throughout the Park, the pathway through the Tree of Life Gardens provides one of the greatest rewards of all—an up-close-and-personal look at some of the upper reaches of the Tree of Life. At roughly the midpoint of the path, you find yourself in close proximity to some of the most striking pieces of sculpture on the Tree. It takes you up to and under the beginning of a waterfall that (the observant Guest will notice) winds its way from the upper reaches of the Tree, down through the Gardens, into and out of animal habitats, under the walkway into the lotus pond at Flame Tree Barbecue, and then out into Discovery Lake. It appears to be a steady stream, but is actually a series of individual water systems that allow the special effects to function while meeting the standards for the Life Support Water systems that are required in animal areas.

Also of note is the organization of the animal sculptures that form the surface of the Tree and its root system. Some animals are rendered large, others small, and some are in herds. There is a great depth to the design—within the roots we see a larger accumulation of insects, and there are areas where the bark has been peeled away, revealing the images of dinosaur fossils, just as they would normally be found when they are dug on land.

Uniquely Unusual

The animals found in the area around the Tree of Life are intended to stimulate thought about the capacity of nature to generate unique and wonderful animal forms, so they are rather unusual animals. We see the largest rodent on earth, the capybara, as well as tiny primates such as the cotton-topped tamarin, and view unusually developed bird specimens. The spotted deer and the kangaroo are beautiful and thought-provoking at the same time. All these and more make us think about the various elements and forces that give animals their shapes.

In keeping with the vision for Discovery Island to be an artistic expression of Man's love for animals, the information on the signposts in these gardens is presented in rhyme. These poetic passages contain real and valuable information about the animals in terms of habitats and food sources, but do so in a way that is itself an artistic expression. The complementary imagery is presented as interpretive artwork as opposed to photography or overly clinical illustration. It all serves to demonstrate the human capacity for admiration of animals.

I Spy with My Dozens of Bug Eyes...

Close, medium, and long shots of the special view ports left behind in the roof structure in the Tree of Life Gardens

One of the most frequently overlooked details in all of Animal Kingdom is this special little gem hidden near the outset of the path through the Tree of Life Gardens. In this little shady spot off to the side of the former queue for *It's Tough To Be A Bug!*, follow the little trails bored in the roots by all of the bugs who've passed this way before. You'll see that several of the paths that pass all the way through set up views for you directly aligned to specific feature animals on the face of the Tree of Life. Just the kind of thing to make sure our Honorary Bugs are never bored themselves!

Spotting a Pattern

Shopping Spree

Elevation of Disney Outfitters by Dave Minichiello

The shops located within Discovery Island are each designed around a specified poetic grouping of animals. This is a design motif that lends the spaces a certain cohesiveness and offers the designers a basis for making their choices.

• Creature Comforts features animals and insects with spots or stripes, such as zebras, tigers, and bumblebees. This even carries outside the store to the ladybug lamp fixture and the cheetahs on the ridgelines of the roof of the cupola.

• Island Mercantile offers a collection of animals that migrate, such as geese, or work, such as beavers and camels.

• When we enter Beastly Bazaar, we are greeted by animals that live in or spend significant time in the water—fish, otters, bears, and more. Outside, there's a carved wooden sea horse framing the walkway in front of the shop.

• Disney Outfitters is decorated wth animals that travel in herds, as indicated by the elephants and rhinoceroses that anchor the large compass lighting fixture.

Elevation of Creature Comforts interior by Karen Connolly Armitage

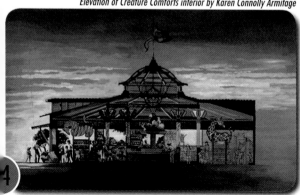

Butterfly with propeller at Island Mercantile

Spotted and striped animals adorn the Creature Comforts roof.

Even on the marquee for Island Mercantile, the working animals get into the act. The beavers and donkeys are a hint of what's in store for you once you go inside.

This turtle, playfully filling the space between the column, the beam, and the bracket at Beastly Bazaar, is an example of how motifs are integrated into the architecture. They will never be dropped into place without regard for their context. This gives them a connection to their environment within our village.

Fixtures of all sorts play out the spots and stripes motif at Creature Comforts.

Support column of carved herd animals at Disney Outfitters

4

Real Craftsmanship

The Imagineers oversee the production of Park motifs in Bali.

If You Want Something Done Right, Go to the Right People

Much of Animal Kingdom is defined by a design standpoint taken from folk-art traditions or by the unique look of work by native artisans who have built and decorated their architecture and artifacts for centuries. While Africa and especially Asia are absolutely dependent upon the faithful re-creation of the ornately carved surfaces and architectural details, the look for Discovery Island was to be a new interpretation of international folk-art styles.

As the aesthetic for the Park was to be an authentic one, it made great sense to go right to the source of the original work and have the actual craftspeople involved in the fabrication of the Park. Working from Imagineering concept sketches, but with a degree of liberty to offer their own interpretations, skilled artists from places such as Nepal, Bali, Java, and Mexico produced practically every bit of carved wood and stone found throughout our lands. There were pieces that were found and purchased and others that were very carefully commissioned to be produced for us in overseas locations, but all have the feeling that can only come from authenticity.

Oaxacan wood carvings adorn the walls of Pizzafari.

An Extended Business Trip

So much production of decorative elements for the Park was being conducted in various Asian countries that in addition to the scouting and purchasing trips, Prop Designer Ken Gomes was sent to live in Bali for the duration of the build, amounting to nearly two years. This was the only way to provide oversight, art direction, tracking, and shipping functions for such a large body of work.

The overseas production effort was extensive and integral to the Park.

During his stay abroad, Ken traveled the country and neighboring territories in search of day-to-day items that would flesh out some of the backdrops for Asia, and worked with vendors to interpret drawings and approve samples. He commissioned the Javanese fishing boats floating in the river behind Drinkwallah. He identified all of the architectural motifs of Discovery Island so that they could be assigned to the proper facilities in order to be correctly applied. There are many elements in the Park that were purchased on the spot from citizens on the street just going about their business. The Imagineers working on-site would periodically receive grab-bag bundles of propping in addition to the carefully identified pieces that already had assigned destinations. It is through the dedicated efforts of these designers that Disney's Animal Kingdom achieves the texture and veracity of detail that is its hallmark.

Bicycle purchased on the streets of Bali

Enlightening Headwear

One of the lead lighting designers on the project team professed a playful theory that a character lighting fixture is not truly a character lighting fixture unless one could wear it on one's head. He maintained a collection of photos of himself wearing an example of each style of light when it showed up on-site. You can only imagine what he might have looked like with these ladybug lamps on his head!

Rocks for Brains

The rockwork at Disney's Animal Kingdom truly established a new state of the art upon its debut. Taking their cue from Imagineering art direction legend Fred Joerger, the WDI sculptors on the team lived by his credo as stated during the construction of Magic Kingdom Park: "If you want to sculpt a rock, you have to *think* like a rock!"

Rockwork framing the entrance to the Otter exhibit on Discovery Island

A Snail's Pace

Much thought went into the placement of the animal motifs throughout Discovery Island. This bench, for example, derives its relaxing nature from the animals placed on the pedestals at each end. The two statues, by different artists in differing styles, are of snails—just the right reference for a place to sit to watch the world pass by.

A Friendly Face

This gorilla, at more than 2,500 pounds, was one of the heaviest of the sculpted motifs brought onto the island. He was so heavy that the straps that were used to lift him into place actually chipped away a little corner of each ear—prompting the construction crew to name him after a well-known boxer whose ear had suffered a similar fate.

Home, Tweet Home

There is a constant effort on the part of Disney's Animal Programs and Imagineering to provide habitats and enrichments for our animals that ensure comfort and a very high quality of life. The bird habitats found on Discovery Island fit the bill nicely. They were designed to meet many different needs for their inhabitants—both physical and psychological. They provide shelter from the sun and rain by way of

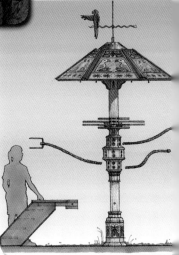

Elevation of parrot habitat and enrichment system by Alex Wright

the colorful canopy, and inside is a heating element that protects them against chilly temperatures. The "branches" and their feeding dishes are interchangeable, so that they can be rearranged daily in order to offer up the variety necessary to prevent boredom on the part of these highly intelligent animals. They provide pathways to explore and points of attachment for the many enrichment devices that are given to the birds. Lastly, another aspect of the design allows us to avoid visual clutter in the Park environment—the stepladder used by the Animal Care staff is custom-built to be easy to mount to the central column and roll offstage out of sight when not in use.

Pizzafari

Peacock mural by Frank Armitage

Rooms with Views

The walls of Pizzafari are adorned with a series of extraordinary murals, and each has a story to tell. These spectacular pieces of art are the work of legendary Disney artist Frank Armitage, who was coaxed out of retirement for this task. Each room is graced by the presence of a different collection of animals that share some categorical theme that ties them together.

The food service area is adorned with the images of ornamental animals—peacocks, parrots, butterflies, and fancy fish. The dining room (behind you when you order) features animals that hang upside-down such as opossums, bats, and snakes. When you enter the hallway to the rear of the building, you are treated to a collection of Oaxacan wood carvings of fantastically patterned animals in numerous combinations. The room to the left is populated with animals that carry their houses—turtles, snails, kangaroos, and such. To the right is the room for nocturnal animals. Its owls, wolves, and raccoons stare back at us through the night. Straight ahead, if you can *spot* them, you'll see animals that camouflage themselves in their habitats. There are leopards, tigers, deer, and polar bears, with all their almost-invisible friends. See if you can find the birds hidden in the grass.

Pizzafari corner bracket motif design by Jenna Goodman

Ants and anteaters at Flame Tree Barbecue

A Tasty Treat

Flame Tree Barbecue has its basis in a traditional Balinese water garden and offers one of the most tranquil spots for enjoying a meal in all of Animal Kingdom. It offers wonderful views of Discovery Lake and across the water toward Asia, including Expedition Everest. This staging owes something to the original plan for the site. Initially, this location was to house an open-air amphitheater with that great view of the lake. When the decision was made to put a show into the Tree of Life rather than the Roots Restaurant, the amphitheater made way for another restaurant concept to meet the needs of the Guests.

There is a delicious irony to the array of architectural motifs that adorn the shade structures and other fixtures of this area. Notice that each of the pairs of animals on a given structure (ants and anteaters, snakes and mice, spiders and bugs) represents a predator-and-prey relationship. This even extends to the decoration of the tables and chairs. The tables are adorned with prey animals and the chairs with predators, so that as you sit to eat, your position in the food chain is made clear. In this way, we are all connected in the great Circle of Life.

Details of predator and prey motifs

Designing for Animals

A Painted Stork enjoys his Imagineer-made environment on the banks of Discovery River.

You Learn Something New Every Day

For each Park, Imagineers encounter new challenges. For Disney's Animal Kingdom, we had to learn a whole new realm of design—that of designing for animals. We needed to learn about animals' needs, capabilities, habits, and the assortment of activities and environmental details that enrich their lives. When we enter this sort of exploration, we study existing examples very closely, we ask lots of questions, we challenge the prevailing assumptions, and we work to develop our own way of looking at a given problem. Our design team spent years working with the preeminent experts in the field of zoological care and facility design, as well as with the top-notch Animal Programs team that was assembled within The Walt Disney Company. The merging of their expertise with our design approach and foundations in storytelling brought a new viewpoint to the world of animal exhibit design. This work has been noted throughout the field and has established new expectations and set new standards in the field of zoological design.

Siamangs in Asia find many places to swing and explore.

Habitat, Sweet Habitat

When we begin a design for any animal habitat at Disney's Animal Kingdom, our primary considerations are the comfort and well-being of the animals and the safety of our Guests. We achieve this by making the habitats as naturalistic and as similar to their native environments as possible. The plant life, the nature and quality of the terrain, the amount of sunlight, and the space available to roam are all part of this equation. We look for opportunities to design enrichment devices that will give the animals something to play on or with in order to stimulate their brains, provide an outlet for physical activities, and add to their quality of life.

We next consider the viewing opportunities we want to make available to our Guests. We try to create appropriate sight lines to allow adequate visibility, while using clever barriers and screening to keep the animal in its preferred location. Our tools of this trade include fencing of various types, moats, water or landscape barriers, underwater bollards, glass panels, and other devices—hidden so as to be invisible to the Guests and therefore not intrude on our story.

The choices we make are based on maintaining our story. For example, lions lend themselves to being seen in a drive-by situation, as on a safari. Deer need to be seen up close and personal. Elephants have requirements that necessitate a great deal of space. We have geographically based story considerations in Africa and Asia, and story conceits in Discovery Island and Oasis that transcend geography.

In order to keep the animals where they can best be seen, it is the practice of WDI and Disney's Animal Programs to provide the most attractive and comfortable "onstage" areas possible. Modifications are made when initial designs prove less than successful. Most of the animals have areas within their habitats that allow them to go "off-stage." For example, our Kilimanjaro Safaris lions (who originated from a zoo in Oregon) initially had difficulty with the Florida heat and spent much time in the cooling shade of the environment's moat—away from Guests' view. So we added air-conditioning to the rock at the front of the lions' promontory, and now they're much more regularly visible. Other lessons learned included the necessity of developing a shroud to avoid exposing our animals to the heat from ground-mounted uplights in Oasis and Discovery Island; splitting the cheetah yard into two sections so that all four animals could be onstage at once; and using colored lighting in backstage spaces to aid our animal keepers' visibility to an expectant gorilla without disturbing her sleep cycle.

CAMP MINNIE-MICKEY

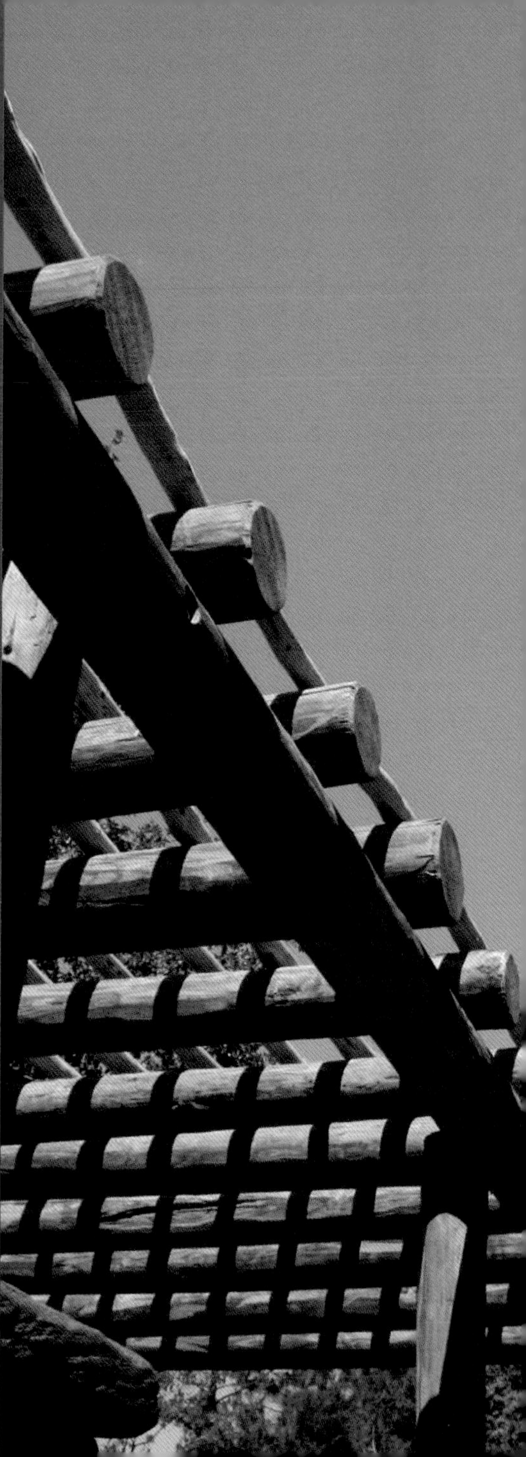

Camp Minnie-Mickey takes us back to the days of our earliest introductions to animals. Here we are free to tap into our childhood mythologies—in which animals are walking, talking friends—where there's nobody with whom we'd rather spend our time. It's always summer vacation here!

Concept by Joe Warren illustrating the relaxing nature of Camp Minnie-Mickey

What a Character!

Camp Minnie-Mickey is the place where our beloved Disney friends go for vacation. It's a summer camp—the kind of place where hiking and fishing fill the days and campfires and storytelling fill the nights. The style of Camp Minnie-Mickey looks like something out of an animated short with the feel of the camping cartoons starring Mickey, his nephews, and Goofy, or the Donald Duck shorts featuring J. Audobon Woodlore and Humphrey Bear.

Within the structure of the themes of Animal Kingdom, Camp Minnie-Mickey represents fictional creatures and our tendency to anthropomorphize animals. Disney has produced a great deal of work that takes advantage of these human characteristics. From the earliest classic animated shorts featuring Mickey Mouse and all of his pals to the greatest of the animated features such as *The Lion King* and *101 Dalmatians*, animals have played primary roles in some of our most popular efforts. While the Disney animated characters are based on real animals, they certainly don't behave exactly like them. We use these animals to illustrate human archetypes and so assign traits that have no real meaning in the animal world to these characters.

For many children, particularly in this day of home entertainment and the availability of the classic Disney films, these animal friends are their first introduction to animals. They represent a softer, more approachable image of the animals than would be portrayed in a nature documentary. Through this process, children learn something about the animals without being intimidated by them.

Another view by Joe Warren of the central stream that defines Camp Minnie-Mickey

*Wood*n't It Be Lovely?

Our Camp Minnie-Mickey is set in the Adirondack Mountains of upstate New York. This heavily wooded, lake-strewn mountain range has been a favorite vacation spot for generations, and over time developed a distinctive style of architectural ornamentation, furniture, and arts and crafts known as Adirondack style. All of the decorative ornamentation in our camp is very deliberate, and the style of architecture works very well with the folk-art derivation of much of the rest of the Park. Adirondack style draws heavily upon the surrounding terrain for its stonework and liberal application of carved wood. The stone provides a very naturalistic foundation for the heavier components of the architecture, while the wood is used in a rustic manner that doesn't strip away too much of its natural beauty. The forms of the wood still show their natural branching and curvature, are often left with their bark for texture, and are only modified when absolutely necessary. Through this approach, the overall impression is that of nature having grown into these forms of its own accord, rather than being altered and shaped by human hands.

Character vignettes like these set the relaxed tone for the land.

Performance Design

Scenic design concept by Joe Warren

To ensure the defined design parameters and merge our high standards for animal care with the high expectations our Guests have for the Disney show, most aspects of Disney's Animal Kingdom require a focused collaboration between WDI and Animal Programs. The theatrical presentation "Pocahontas & Her Forest Friends" is an example of an effort that necessitated even more of that cooperation than others. The engaging animal behaviors could not be featured without it.

This show, which features Pocahontas as a hostess who introduces us to her animal friends, was developed by WDW Creative Entertainment in partnership with Animal Programs. It presents an important message of conservation through Pocahontas's efforts to preserve her friends' homes. She is assisted by the sage advice of Grandmother Willow and the enthusiastic contributions of Sprig, the little sapling. The message carries a great deal of impact due to the presence of the live and engaging woodland animals that give the story a connection to the real world.

WDI supports this sort of effort by developing and building the required facilities, both onstage and in backstage support structures. In order to design a performance space for the animals, we need to have a great understanding of the needs of the animals and the behaviors that the Animal Care staff intended to spotlight. Above all, the safety and comfort of the animals in their backstage housing is paramount. There is a great deal of planning put into the placement of entrances, the angle of ramps, and the means of containment so that the flow of the show can be maintained and the timing preserved. We have to be cognizant of all materials placed on the surfaces in order to provide grip but not retain heat, and any finishes that could potentially be ingested by the animals.

Critter Country

"Pocahontas & Her Forest Friends" offers our furry cast an opportunity to introduce themselves in person after all these years of helping to carry our stories as lead and supporting characters in many Disney animated films. The traits and tendencies put on display by our highly observant animators are used as the basis for this charming stage show. Through the dialogue of Pocahontas, Grandmother Willow, and Sprig—intermingled with cameo appearances by the animals—we highlight the various woodland creatures and gain a little understanding of each one's special nature. Our Animal Programs team looked for just the right behaviors to showcase—as consistently as can be expected from these actors—then worked with Entertainment and WDI to develop a script around them.

Theater plan by Jim Heffron

Ridin' the Rails to Work

The theater has a very shallow space between the top of the stage and the floor of the foundation down below. In order to move the puppeteer into position to operate Sprig, the Imagineers had to think a little differently about how to move somebody around. In this case, the puppeteer climbs into a custom-built "go-kart" with a reclining seat. Lying flat on the cart, the performer travels on rails toward the final position under the rock by pulling his or her way along a ladder mounted underneath the stage floor.

Concept sketch used to develop puppeteer access by Alex Wright

5

The Personal Touch

Concept for character meeting place by Alex Wright

The character greeting areas in the woods around Camp Minnie-Mickey each have a distinctive look, which determines the assortment of characters likely to be encountered there. There is a woodland venue, a jungle-y one, one with a storybook feel, and another that is more connected to the look of the camp itself. This gives each character a bit of context that's appropriate to the setting in which it is typically presented, but the palette of materials is consistent throughout so that all of the gazebos work within the styling of the land.

Read the Signs

Our land marquees are more than just directional devices that help people find their way around the Park. They are the first opportunity we have to begin to tell the story of the land, through visual styling and design communication. The marquee for Camp Minnie-Mickey evokes the character of the land—it is nestled into a heavily wooded setting and built with a very rustic construction of hand-hewn materials, with the Adirondack wood styling featured very prominently. The character silhouettes on the metalwork complete the message.

Trickle-down Effect

The stream that greets you as you enter the land is an important element of the placemaking here. Taking a look up the hill at the babbling brook meandering through this forest, it's difficult to believe that you're not really in the Adirondacks. The creation of a natural feature like this is no small feat as live stone is merged with carved rockwork, the landscape is laid out to integrate realistically with the terrain, and then the water flow system is designed and tuned by our Special Effects team.

Find Your Path

Sometimes we have to make modifications to our parks, simply in the interest of improving their functionality. Over the first several years of the operation of Disney's Animal Kingdom, it became apparent that the show "Festival of the Lion King" was a huge hit and was not about to slow down, so we had to make accomodations to handle the large crowds as they exited the theater. In Camp Minnie-Mickey, we also have to maintain the comfortable and intimate scale of the land, so we can't always take a particular thing and just blow it up to a larger scale. Sometimes an object loses its identity if it expands beyond the scale that is meant for it. In the case of the bridge adjacent to the Lion King Theater, it meant designing an additional canopied bridge with its own design motif rather than just widening the existing footbridge. In this way, we added the pathway we needed without creating a large expanse that would be out of character for the land.

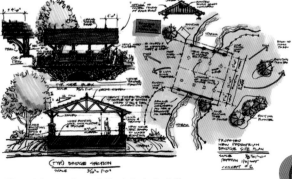

Plan and elevations for new bridge design by Jim Heffron

Festival of the Lion King

Camp-side Circle of Life

Festival of the Lion King

"Festival of the Lion King" has been one of the most popular shows in all of the Disney theme parks. Developed by WDW Creative Entertainment, this show tells the story of a traveling troupe led by some of our favorite characters from the animated film *The Lion King*. These friends have come to Camp Minnie-Mickey to share their music and dance and other skills with all the campers.

Imagineering's involvement was limited primarily to the design of the performance venue. We started with the story of Camp Minnie-Mickey and tried to ascertain how a stage show would fit into the world of a summer camp. The best option available for the gathering of a large group is the camp's assembly hall, where all the campers come together to sing songs and tell stories. This led us to our material and color palettes, and the architectural styling of the building.

Bill Evans and Paul Comstock on-site

The Seeds of Good Design

From the earliest days of Disneyland, legendary Imagineer Bill Evans developed the techniques that would come to define the WDI approach to landscape design. It was an entirely new mode of thinking that treated the landscape elements of the parks as extensions of the sets—a very theatrical aesthetic. Nearly fifty years later, Disney's Animal Kingdom was fortunate enough to benefit from Bill's hand in its planning and development. Just as we do with our sets, however, we have to modify our design approach with landscape to connect to the story we are trying to tell. Bill and his disciples, including Animal Kingdom's lead landscape designer, Paul Comstock, knew the Park would call for the landscaping to play a very different role.

In our other parks, the landscape tends to fall into one of the following categories:

- A beautiful, decorative extension of the design parameters we've established within a fantastical environment like Tomorrowland
- An abstract design connected to a thematic setting—Future World at Epcot or the load area for "it's a small world" at Disneyland
- A theatrical device complementing a scene that is somewhat realistic, but also stylized to some degree—Jungle Cruise at the Magic Kingdom or Hollywood Boulevard at the Disney Studios

Animal Kingdom requires that the landscape live and breathe and be itself, a real part of a real-world environment. It is not to be managed or manicured in order to give it "beauty." It is to please the eye of the Guest on the basis of its natural beauty. It would be a mistake to interpret that approach as the absence of design—rather it is merely design applied to a different end. The site only retains a few dozen trees from what had been essentially a cow pasture. Practically every bit of plant material you see here has been brought in and planted. The scale and logistics of the effort alone made it one of the largest landscape design efforts ever undertaken.

AFRICA

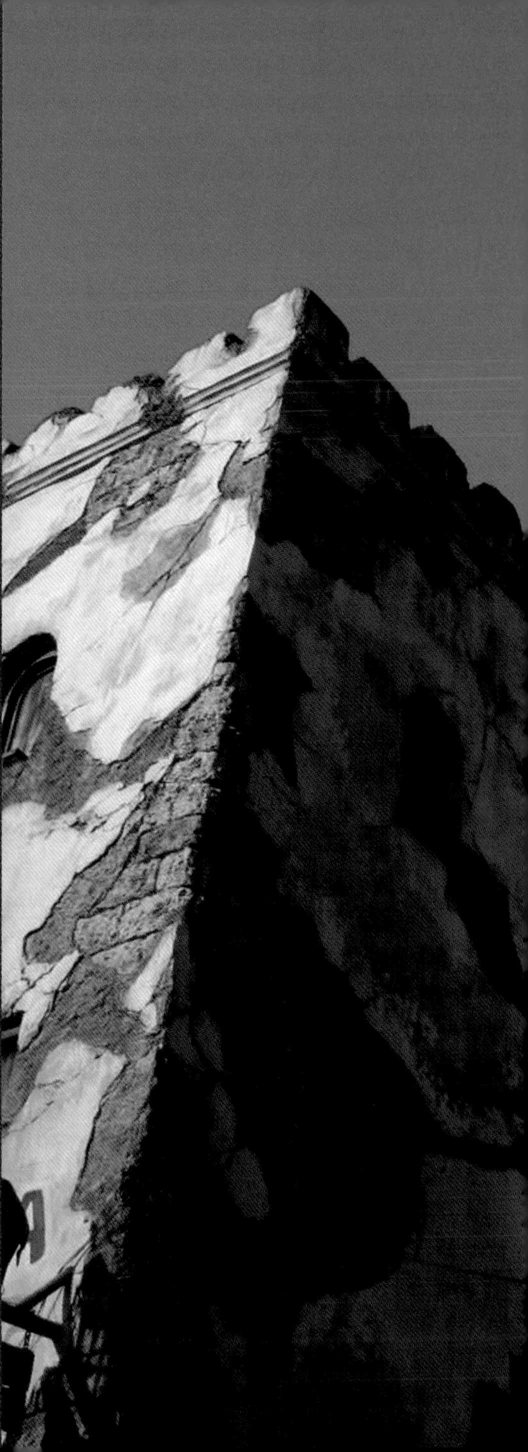

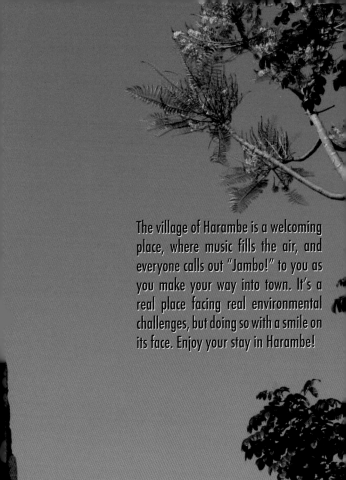

The village of Harambe is a welcoming place, where music fills the air, and everyone calls out "Jambo!" to you as you make your way into town. It's a real place facing real environmental challenges, but doing so with a smile on its face. Enjoy your stay in Harambe!

One Story at a Time

Overall view of Harambe illustrated by Tom Gilleon

Our Africa is not based on any particular place on the continent that it represents, but it feels like many places one can find there. Welcome to Harambe—Swahili for "working together"—our east-coast African fishing village. There's a very specific reason that the choice was made to portray this particular version of African life—storytelling. In order to achieve dramatic impact with the stories we wanted to create, we have to focus on one story at a time. Here, it is that of Nature as a pristine thing with animals that must be protected from poaching.

Certainly there are places in Nairobi or Lagos or Johannesburg in which one could mistake the setting for any large, modern city around the world. But to focus on that here would be to miss the point—this story is about animals, not humans. While a cultural backdrop adds detail and enriches the experience, the core story line only deals with human development to the extent that it affects the animal kingdom.

When you want to tell a story about animals, you have to go to the places where the real decisions are being made—the frontlines in the conservation debate, where the real impact can be made in the near future. Here in Harambe, we're in a place very much like many places in Africa where people really do live right on the edge of the wilderness, winin close proximity of real wildlife.

Another reason we created a fictitious place is that it allowed us to avoid becoming linked to the political history of any specific country. We use the design of Harambe to imply its history. Similarly, Swahili was chosen as the language of Harambe because it crosses geographic boundaries. It is important for this place to have a history, but equally important that it not get in the way of the animal story we're here to see and hear.

A Guided Tour of Harambe

The role of the Guest in the story line of Harambe is a believable one. When you walk the streets of this town and are greeted by the residents, you are acting as a tourist who has come to this place, probably because you want to take a safari at the Harambe Wildlife Reserve. The tribal architecture found in much of Africa isn't conducive to theme park function, without resorting to a fantasy version as one might see in Adventureland at Magic Kingdom. The building structures would not afford us the ability to house public spaces, merchandise shops, restaurants, or other practical requirements. This led us to Swahili architecture, a traditional form prevalent in East Africa, with a broad range of building forms. There was a conscious effort not to rely heavily on colonial architectural forms, as these outside influences would take us away from our African story. There are vestiges of the colonial past, however, as in the Portuguese design of the fort—now Tamu Tamu Refreshments—that formed the original boundaries of the first settlement of the town. This fort has fallen into disrepair, but still remains an imposing ediface. The British influence can be seen in the mailboxes and the signs regarding the cattle company indicated on the Safari unload platforms. As in Lamu, Kenya—which served as our primary reference—many of the buildings carry a blue cast in their coloration owing to the fact that in Lamu their white pigments are mixed with laundry bluing in order to make them "whiter." We used pumice blocks on the surface of Tusker House in order to mimic the look of the coral blocks used in Lamu.

There is a very distinct contrast between the urban environment within the town and the nearby savannah in order to highlight the boundary between Man and Animal. Human control is in evidence everywhere. All of the plants are placed in planters and behind hard barriers to illustrate this point.

Aerial view of Kilimanjaro Safaris as illustrated by Tom Gilleon

Kilimanjaro Safaris

Safari so Good

Bird's-eye illustration of the savannah by Ben Tripp

Kilimanjaro Safaris is a central element not only to this land, but also to the backstory of Harambe as an important aspect of the evolution of this place. Our story holds that the Harambe Wildlife Reserve was once a game-hunting reserve, but at some point in the early 1970s—when issues of conservation were coming to the fore—the townspeople made a conscious decision to change the usage of the land. Now it is a preservation zone, with animals available only for photo safaris via guided tours. It was clearly a big decision for the town, with significant potential economic impact, but the collective viewpoint had come around to the point that they felt this was a necessary step.

It is through this backdrop that we view the presence of the poachers who have intruded into the reserve to illegally obtain animals for trade. This story is critical to the conservation messages inherent to all of Animal Kingdom. When we encounter a violation of this place that has been set aside as being protected by an environmentally connected worldview, we feel the sense of loss deeply. The positive resolution of the story indicates to us that we can make a difference in this equation by "growing eyes for poachers."

Conceptual view of animal interactions on the savannah by Ned Mueller

Peekaboo, I Can't...See...You?

Clearly the intent for Kilimanjaro Safaris is for us to be traveling through a natural environment with animals living in their own world, not on display in exhibits for our benefit. This means that our animals are contained via a variety of means that are, for the most part, invisible to the Guest. By applying theatrical sight-line studies to these natural forms—much as we would for any set design in any of our parks—we have created unseen moats, underwater bollards, fences screened by foliage, landscape barriers, and rockwork for containment.

Inspirational art for lion habitat by Nadya Geras-Carson

QUICK TAKES

- Kilimanjaro Safaris, at roughly 110 acres, is almost the same size as the entire Magic Kingdom Park!

- The landscaping for the savannah was one of the earliest projects completed during construction of the Park, in order to give the plant material time to take root before being subjected to all of the animal traffic upon their release into the habitat. The plants were in place for a year to eighteen months prior to animal acclimation.

- The apparently random ruts in the vehicle pathway are actually very carefully designed to keep the "show" water in the road from intermingling with the "life support" water in the animal habitats.

- Many of the flat-topped trees dotting the savannah are not really the African acacias they have been trimmed to resemble, but rather live oak trees with their tops flattened to resemble acacias. Real acacia trees would have had a very difficult time standing up to the constant feeding of all of our giraffes, who don't seem to mind the switch.

An Edible Set

Caption for photo of Safari landscaping

Most scenic designers don't have to deal with the difficulty of a cast eating their set every day. At Kilimanjaro Safaris, that's just what happens. Our landscape architects, who designed and maintain the forests and savannahs of this attraction, use the landscape elements just as a theatrical designer would use scenic flats, props, and backdrops to create the world of their show—with the additional challenges offered up by the animals who would inhabit this stage.

Our landscape designers are used to working with plant material in the service of scenic design, as they have on countless WDI projects dating back to the earliest days of Disneyland, but here the landscape is the entire set rather than a complementary element. It creates every bit of the setting in which we tell this story. The traditional theme-park architecture is limited to the queue, the load and unload buildings, and the backstage animal holding facilities.

The primary function of the landscape design is placemaking. Our Guests and fellow explorers need to feel as though they are halfway around the world and miles away from civilization in order to absorb the story of this show. The landscape team has created multiple spaces, from the relatively cozy confines of the Ituri forest at the outset to the vast vistas of the savannah as the attraction reaches its crescendo.

The next priority for the landscape is the screening of views in order to control the elements of the safari that the Guests are allowed to see. Here the various pieces of the landscapers palette are put to use as purely theatrical devices, with berms, screen walls, landscape barriers, and real and artifical trees blocking our vision and focusing us on the animals we are there to see.

Lastly, our landscapers worked with our expert animal facility design consultants to verify that each habitat conformed to the highest standards in the industry in terms of animal care and safety. They studied each species' jump profile, widths of moats, wall textures, and all the other aspects of a facility that ensure the safe viewing of animals.

What Are You Looking At?

For research for Kilimanjaro Safaris, our designers went on photo safaris in Africa. Certainly the team was excited to see animals when they were visible (far less frequently than on our attraction, they're very proud to point out), but that really wasn't the primary purpose. The Imagineers were there to study the environment, the plants, the rocks, and the roadways. Lead designer John Shields evidently made quite an impression on the guides for one group, when they couldn't understand why he wasn't even paying attention to the animals nearby, but was instead walking around looking at the ground and taking pictures of the dirt! He wanted to capture the look of the tire tracks as they made inpressions in the rutted pathways. That isn't *usually* the goal of the typical tourist at such a place. Our safari's roadway is the result.

Starting From Scratch

Elements captured on those trips were faithfully recreated on-site in Florida. The safari site had been practically cleared to nothing but bare earth. Overall land forms were sculpted per the plans. Plants were brought in after having been grown in special containers, called "accelerators," that allowed them to flourish at a rapid rate so that we could have a more-mature-than-usual collection of plant material to put into the ground well in advance of Opening Day. Certain plants were substituted for others that wouldn't grow well in this climate. Special care was taken to plant the foliage and grasses in random patterns to avoid the appearance of a man-made space.

The physical animal barriers were laid out and intermingled into the landscape design, with bodies of water, faux mud banks, and hidden fences serving to contain the stars of this show. Feeders were hidden into the landscape, placed inside fallen logs, behind rocks, and even into the cradles of the large baobob trees. Everything had to be engineered to withstand the elements and the animals. Most of these elements had to be fabricated rather than planted, along with the rock outcroppings, the roadway itself, and special details scattered throughout the reserve to make it believable. Your safari guide will tell you that termite mounds are as hard as concrete. And it's true...especially ours!

A History Lesson

The engraving on the surface of this bench—Uhuru 1961—illustrates an element of the history that has been created for Harambe. The Swahili word "Uhuru" means "freedom." The dating on this bench refers to an important political change that took place that year, and ties into all of the decisions subsequently made during its development since. The unspecified freedom gained during the fictional events of 1961 put the decision-making in the hands of the people of Harambe, allowing for the rethinking of the town's economic development and interaction with its natural surroundings.

That'll Leave a Mark

If you take a look at the paving at the entry to Harambe near the corner ice-cream stand, you'll see the remnants of the old city walls. According to our history, Harambe was once surrounded by a fortress perimeter, but the only remaining signs are the footprints of the old walls in the dirt. This layering of history, while subtle, informs our perception of the age of a place.

No Time Like the Present

It is very important that it be clear to our Guests that the Harambe we've chosen to present to them is fully a part of the modern world. The new power lines strewn about over the top of the old buildings, the "Computer Training" graphic on the wall, and the satellite dishes on the rooftops tell this part of our story perfectly for us.

Can I Get You Some Eggs with That Sausage?

At the end of Mombasa Marketplace you'll find a rather curious-looking plant with long, hanging fruit in the shape of a sausage. Coincidentally enough, it's called a sausage tree. This specialty tree brought in by our landscape designers required special care from the Park horticulture team to produce its fruit without the bats that pollinate them in Africa.

Name Game

Imagineers love to plant references to the members of the project teams in the parks. If you look closely at the graphics in Harambe, you'll find references to creative lead Joe Rohde, landscape planner John Shields, and architect Ahmad Jafari. There's even a sly mention of an Imagineer who left the company during the project.

Pangani Forest Exploration Trail

Sketch of Research Station by Mark Shumate

We're in Training

Pangani Forest Exploration Trail is a walking attraction that takes the form of a training facility where researchers and volunteers are taught conservation techniques that they will apply at the Harambe Wildlife Reserve or elsewhere in Africa or the world. It is indicated on the marquee that this site is administered by the Reserve itself. Here we see what the researchers see as we look at the animals through viewing blinds, research facilities, and observation portals.

Through this story, we are able to impart information to our Guests through three means. There are some locations arranged as classroom setups where researchers gather for further education and at which we find chalkboards and visual aids that have been put there by the instructors. In other places we encounter field notes left behind or left for one another by researchers. Lastly, we have the representatives from Animal Programs, who in this instance portray the researchers themselves and are available to Guests who have questions or just want to listen to the stories of this place.

Pangani means "place of enchantment" in Swahili, and the lush and inviting environs planted and built by the Imagineers for this attraction certainly fit that description. Interesting details for the observant researcher include specific animal footprints that you can find imprinted on the dirt paths, the masking of the entry to the aviary, the steady drip coming through the leaky wall in the Hippo-viewing building, and the faux bamboo filling the last opening in the rockwork at the gorilla exhibit.

74

Creature Feature

The featured habitat is that of the gorillas, which can be viewed from several vantage points on this pathway as well as from an overlook near the unload platform for Kilimanjaro Safaris. The observation station at which they are first encountered imparts much of the learning gathered by the researchers. Once inside the gorillas' realm, we find ourselves on a suspension bridge and then on an island with a view to each side into the family and bachelor groups. This puts us at eye level with these amazing creatures, while maintaining all of the required safety and containment protocols. The waterfall on the family side was added as an enrichment for the gorillas after the Park opened, offering them a source of cool water in which to take a drink, play, or simply cool off.

Inspirational paintings by Nadya Geras-Carson explore the world of the animals from their point of view. Note that the gorilla image below presumes that the gorilla habitat would be part of the safari experience rather than the walking trail that would

eventually become Pangani Forest. It is not uncommon for ideas to be moved around from place to place during the development of a park concept. It is only through this sort of exploration that we land upon the very best solution for a given design or story challenge.

Timely Termites

During the Park's construction, Imagineering sculptor Eric Miller was assigned the task of sculpting this termite mound, but only as a "fill-in" job to complete as he had time in between stints on some of his bigger projects. He reported on his progress over the course of several months. At the next team meeting after finishing the piece, he proudly announced that it had taken him only a little longer than it takes...termites.

Wildlife Express Train

Concept for the intent of the Harambe Train Station by Zofia Kostyrko

All Aboard!

Our first glimpse of the back-of-house spaces of Disney's Animal Kingdom occurs when we climb aboard the Wildlife Express Train to Rafiki's Planet Watch. It is important to WDI and Animal Programs that Guests are offered some insight into the effort required to maintain the animal population of the Park and the care with which we approach this responsibility. In the very earliest planning sessions, it was determined that the animal facilities of Animal Kingdom—both onstage and off—would be designed and built to the most exacting standards within the entire industry, and that our Guests should have visibility into this caring environment.

Our trip on the Wildlife Express run of the Eastern Star Railway begins in Harambe. The station carries the look of travel in the developing world, with propping and environmental graphics that set the scene and tell the story of this part of the world. This station and the trains probably date from some time in the colonial past of Harambe, perhaps in the 1920s or 1930s, with more recent additions by the town showing up in the thatched-roof wings that cover the load areas. The train has not been replaced or upgraded because there is no need to—in the developing world, nothing is wasted. The residents of a place like Harambe don't have that luxury, so an item that we might consider junk would still be seen as having value here and would continue to be put to good use. The train is still there because it still runs.

Along the 1.2 mile route, we see into the housing facilities for our lions, rhinoceroses, elephants, warthogs, cheetahs, and gazelles. We can see how these buildings relate to the onstage components of Kilimanjaro Safaris. The facilities are built with the needs of the animals and the Animal Care staff in mind. There are comfortable spaces with no sharp edges, sufficient structure for containment, access for the daily veterinary assessments, and enrichment devices to make the lives of the residents more enjoyable. Note the variations in building size and style relative to the species being housed there.

Illustration of Wildlife Express train by George McGinnis

We've Got a Train to Match!

Trains make excellent devices to indicate time and place, as their designs over the years have been so distinctive. Oddly enough, however, it's difficult to find real and reliably operable early-20th-century trains. So, we had to design one for ourselves and figure out a way to get it built. This kind of specialty fabrication is frequently required when we build Disney theme parks, so Imagineers are experts at finding suitable manufacturers and working with them to deliver the finished pieces. These efforts can take us anywhere in the world.

Though they appear to be quite old, the three engines and two sets of cars of the Eastern Star Railway were actually built in 1997. They were manufactured to our design specifications only a few miles from William Shakespeare's cottage in Stratford-upon-Avon, England. The Eastern Star Railway joins the long list of Disney railroads installed at Disney parks around the world since the original at Disneyland, all owing to Walt's lifelong fascination with trains.

Paint elevation for Wildlife Express locomotive

WARDS DE OOS-U3

SINCLAIR SIN8782

NOTE: COLORS INDIC/

ENTIRE VEHICLE TO

PER OWNER ART DI

7

Rafiki's Planet Watch offers a behind-the-scenes look at animal-care tasks around the Park and at conservation efforts going on all around the world. Here, Guests can take the next step toward acquiring a greater depth of knowledge and a plan of action for getting involved. This is where Animal Kingdom extends beyond its berm.

Home Run

Concept for entrance to Conservation Station by Zofia Kostyrko

Rafiki's Planet Watch is where the themes of Disney's Animal Kingdom connect back to the world in which our Guests live. Here they are offered optimistic, positive conservation messages meant to instill hope that change can be effected, and knowledge as to how an individual can participate in that change. We hear about the work done by real conservationists around the world—some of whom began their efforts simply as concerned citizens rather than trained professionals.

It's important that this part of the Park, with its windows into the real world, tell stories that provide great examples of successes. Here we equip any Guest who is so inclined with the tools and knowledge—or pathways to follow for further knowledge—that will allow them to take action in solving the challenges facing our environment.

The messages are imparted from the moment we start down the pathway from the train station to Conservation Station and deal with issues and possibilities from one's own backyard to some of the most remote reaches of this planet. They range from small-scale individual efforts to macro issues involving the actions of entire human populations.

Railway Transportation To

PLANET WATCH

Open Your Eyes To The World Around You

This design concept illustration for the marquee for Rafiki's Planet Watch by Jason Renfroe illustrates the means of transition from the realism of Harambe to the stylization of this land.

What Does Optimism Look Like?

The styling of Rafiki's Planet Watch and all of the associated structures allows us to believe that anything is possible, and that positive change is within our reach. So the colors are bold and bright and cheerful, the shapes and patterns playful and childlike. Images of animals are everywhere, presented in a more realistic fashion than almost anywhere else in the Park—with less human interpretation. Even the abstracted animal forms that appear in silhouette on fences or in paving patterns are taken in a much more literal direction artistically. The animals are here to tell you their story themselves. All of the information given is very important and correct, but the environment in **which it is conveyed** is intentionally upbeat.

Animal graphics greet you at Conservation Train Station

Marquee mural by John Rowe from a design by Zofia Kostyrko

81

Cotton-topped tamarins show you their backyards.

Hometown Conservation

Habitat Habit, a series of exhibits found along the path to Conservation Station, truly brings the idea of conservation to our backyards, wherever they may be. These displays show us how we can make our own spaces more hospitable for the animals with whom we share our neighborhoods. The exhibits, which have been registered as certified Backyard Habitats through the National Wildlife Federation, demonstrate methods of dealing with trash, wood piles, water elements, animal feeders, and animal houses in ways that make the environments more pleasant for us as well as for our fuzzy friends.

We see butterfly gardens and bat houses. We get to look at some ideas for the arrangement of fountains or ponds that might offer water for birds or grow plants that are welcoming for fish or frogs or toads. We learn about integrated pest management, illustrated by daily ladybug releases. All of these practices and techniques help us to work toward a more integrated environment for both humans and animals to share. It enriches the relationship for both sides. What could be closer to the heart of the mission of Disney's Animal Kingdom than that?

Stamp of Approval

In order to certify a backyard habitat through the National Wildlife Federation, the site must provide each of the four basic elements that any animal needs for survival: food, water, shelter, and a place to raise young. Once certified, a habitat joins the national registry, and is eligible to display a sign proclaiming its value in our local ecosystems. This program is available to any Guest if he or she is interested.

Something's Afoot!

As you make your way up the path, look at the pavement under each of the pavilions, and you'll see a story progression right under your feet. At each stop, there are several animal and tree motifs sculpted into the walkway. At the first pavilion, they are scattered around seemingly unaware of each other. By the second canopy, the elements have begun to work their way together. At the end of the trail just before you reach Conservation Station, you'll see a medallion imprinted into the pathway in which the pieces have come together to form a poetic image of the Circle of Life, with all the creatures of the Earth intertwined with nature in a singular form, each one dependent upon the others.

Concept of Conservation Station interior by Zofia Kostyrko

Eco, Eco, Eco...

Conservation Station is the nerve center of Disney's Animal Kingdom, and the center of The Walt Disney Company's global commitments to the environment and to animal conservation. Again, the emphasis is on positive environmental success stories from around the world. We use appropriate Disney characters, whose voices lend themselves to this subject matter, to talk us through some of the messages we deliver. For example, Rafiki is a fitting spokescharacter because his identity is that of a wise and worldly creature, well suited to talking about the impact of our actions upon the environment and the consequences that then fall upon the animal population. Pocahontas—being very much in touch with nature and the creatures who live there—is the perfect one to take us there in Song of the Rainforest.

This is also the place where the Animal Programs effort is based. There is much that can be learned here about the effort required to operate Animal Kingdom. We have views throughout the Park via the Animal Cams, and can see into the veterinary labs to learn about the care given to our residents. We use voice-recognition technology to simulate conversations between Guests and several real-world Eco-Heroes. There is also an academic side to the Park, and much of that work is focused here with classrooms behind the scenes where this work is disseminated.

FOLLOW THE CONSERVATION TRAIL
FROM YOUR HOMETOWN ZOO
TO THE WILD WORLD

Eco Web touts the possibilities of modern communications technologies such as the Internet to connect people to conservation initiatives around the world.

84

Through the Looking Glass

One of the most important elements of Conservation Station is the view it offers into the function of the veterinary services offered to our animals at Disney's Animal Kingdom. It was determined early on that the policies regarding animal care here would have to be very open and highly visible. It is through this effort that we ensure that any practices we develop will be made available to the broader zoological community, and that we can maintain the reputation for animal care that allows us to participate in breeding programs and receive animals on loan from other facilities. We also want it to be quite evident to our Guests that all of our animals receive the highest level of care that we can possibly give them. It's a fascinating opportunity for Guests to see an exam or a surgery. The ability that the veterinarians have to converse with the audience adds to that experience. Other views into laboratory spaces and food prep kitchens round out this peek behind the scenes.

Conservation Station graphic from train station

Sketch of veterinary technician by Chris Runco

Early concepts for activities inside Conservation Station by Suzanne Rattigan

85

Touchy Feely

Affection Section is yet another type of reward for the adventurous Guest. We humans have an innate love for animals, which is fed all day long during the rest of the shows and experiences that make up the Park. But for all the animals that one encounters before getting to Affection Section, there are very few opportunities to actually touch them. In the spirit of the rewards that we offer to Guests who choose to explore, the reward found all the way at the northern end of the Park is a chance to indulge our desires to pet an animal.

This experience becomes an important emotional component of the Park story. This chance for actual physical contact brings the value of animals closer than ever. Even though these animals are not of the sort that are facing danger from habitat loss or extinction—as we really don't have the option to offer this kind of contact with those animals—the broader story relative to all animals still comes through. This message is especially valuable for children, and they walk away with a renewed sense of connection to the animal kingdom.

Concept by Zofia Kostyrko for the Affection Section

Now Presenting...

Our outdoor stage at Affection Section is an opportunity for Guests to interact with our Animal Care staff. The shows are fun and playful, and very informative. It's a wonderful opportunity to engage the children and get them to think more about these issues. The presentations offered there daily involve exhibitions of animal behaviors and real animal information, along with a chance to ask questions of the animal keepers. They are able to offer further insights into the operation of the Park. This connects the Guests to the ongoing efforts here at Animal Kingdom, onstage, behind the scenes, and extending out into the world around us. These staff members are enthusiastic ambassadors for the Park and all that it represents.

Set design concept by Alex Wright

Grab your gear and come along for a trek through the jungles and villages of southwest Asia. Our town of Anandapur can be the hub for all of your adventures—hiking through the ruins of a sultan's palace, riding the whitewater of a mountain stream, or braving the face of the tallest mountain on Earth. Asia will provide you with animal encounters you'll never forget.

Illustration by Ray Spencer of the view as one approaches Serka Zong

The West of the Story

The actual continent of Asia demonstrates a long-established pattern of development noteworthy for its unique relationship with the natural environment. There has been a tendency to clear land in such a way as to create patches of jungle within the cities, and patches of city within the jungles. We define our Asia by its animals, not its countries. Our Asia exists without geo-political boundaries. Rather, it is habitat-driven. Anandapur is a mythical town in an unnamed country located in the floodplains and lower foothills of the Himalayas. Sanskrit was chosen as the local language because it is no longer actively spoken, but has influenced the languages of several countries.

We've chosen to stay away from depictions of the dense, modernized populations of China, Japan, or Korea that have created barriers between humans and animals. Instead we went to places where ancient lifestyles can interact with modernization and endangered habitats to create compelling situations. It was also felt that Nepal, India, Thailand, and Indonesia have received relatively little exposure in the West, so they offer potentially more surprising and evocative settings.

Anandapur—Sanskrit for "Place of all delight"—presents a different character than Harambe. Whereas Harambe is essentially an urban setting, highlighting the tendency toward town centers on that continent, Anandapur demonstrates the intermingling of natural spaces and built environments that stretches more or less from one end of Asia to the other. Also, while we do indicate the presence of a civic entity, it is less influential than the one in Harambe. There is a sense of self-government and folksiness here to set it apart from our Africa.

How Do We Get There?

So, what is it that makes this land what it is? How do we achieve the placemaking that is so critical to our ability to tell the stories that we want to tell? How do we impart the spirit of this part of the world that so drew us to it? The answers lie in the details, particularly the ones that make these parts of the world so unique.

We make some choices in order to differentiate each of our lands from a design standpoint. For instance, though bamboo sees widespread use in the real Africa, we confine its use in the Park to Asia so that the two maintain distinct identities to our Guests.

We make other choices in order to link this place to our message. A prayer tree such as the one in the Tiger Tree statue at the land entrance is a common sight along the roadways and trekking trails throughout Asia. The ribbons that you see hanging from the tree each represent a prayer left by a passing traveler—the bells indicate answered prayers. It is believed that to remove the prayer ribbon will invalidate it, so the design guidelines and the Park maintenance directives call for the ribbons to be left in place until they are tattered and simply wither away, just as happens in the real Asia.

The fact that this ancient tree has overtaken the original statue is also an important aspect of this vignette. It's a motif that repeats itself throughout Asia and Anandapur. It is not at all uncommon to find ancient buildings dating back several centuries that have been destroyed from within by trees planted inside at the same time the building was completed. It's a sort of tacit acknowledgment of the futility of attempting to overcome nature. Thematically, this imagery is inextricably linked to the core story lines of the Park.

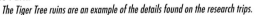

The Tiger Tree ruins are an example of the details found on the research trips.

Concept for an Asian market by Joe Rohde

Have Project, Will Travel

When the project team came to the realization very early on in the development of Animal Kingdom that the design aesthetic would be one of exacting realism, it became clear that they would need to travel extensively in order to capture the essence of the places they would depict in a way that would be truly believable. After the locales of the Park were settled upon, a core team of six or so designers set off to gather the particulars regarding those locales, in order to inform the entire design effort. As the team grew, additional designers made trips, following very specific itineraries to build a shared body of knowledge and ensure that everyone was speaking the same design language.

The locations we chose to depict at this park in order to support our story are not ones that show up frequently in books or architectural studies. In many cases, the only way for us to find extensive information on these places was to go to them. Even if books are available for research into the places we depict, if books are all we work from, we'll only know what other people tell us. It forces us to tell somebody else's story, guided and limited by the choices they've made in deciding what to include in their book. As authors, we want to tell our own stories. We want to speak from a position of authority, via our own experiences.

This building is one that benefitted directly from the learnings gathered by the Everest Team on their travels through Asia.

Souvenirs from Our Travels

So what do Imagineers do on research trips like these? They gather anything and everything that they think will help them to re-create elements from the places they've visited when they return to the Park. We bring back memories from conversations with the people we encounter. We talk about materials and methods of construction that help us determine our production strategies, local customs that might yield propping vignettes or backstories, and histories and traditions that might have shaped a place over time. The important thing is for the designers to absorb not simply what a place looks like, but what it feels like to be there. We have to experience a place for ourselves in order to determine what aspects of a place will forward our stories.

An impression of Asia by Joe Cotter

Certainly there are photos taken. These pictures are cataloged and distributed amongst the rest of the project team in order to glean details and design motifs that we will work into our heightened realities. Our core team's travels in support of Africa and Asia netted several thousand photos from each continent. And this was pre-digital!

Prop designers study the details of the everyday items found within the place and the culture. Character Paint and Plaster designers photograph their reference sources from multiple distances in order to capture just what is in the details of a surface that give it its character in the close, medium, and long shots. They even pull paint chip samples from buildings and other objects and make surface rubbings to capture specific textures from walls or building facades. These serve as templates on the project site. It is very difficult to capture this level of description in written notes or through photography.

Distinctive details such as these crazy power poles were seen every step of the way.

Caravan Stage

Traveling Show

Caravan Stage marquee concept elevation by Joe Rohde

Before entering Asia proper we encounter Caravan Stage. This open-air performance space, the home of the bird show Flights of Wonder, is appropriate as a transitional device. It is designed as something that could be found in the Taklimakan desert of Asia—perhaps along the Silk Road in the area of northern India, southern Russia, Kazakhstan, Turkmenistan, or Tibet—a trade route between northern Africa and the areas of southwest Asia depicted at Animal Kingdom. It is a caravansary— a place for caravans to gather as they stop along the way during their long and arduous travels. It affords us a pleasant diversion and respite as we travel between Africa and Asia at the Animal Kingdom scale. The travelers have laid out their rugs to dry on the roof, lending some much-needed color to the understandably very earth-toned architecture. The marquee at the entrance is cobbled together from found objects that they had on hand.

The architecture is taken from photos brought back during research trips to the Tibetan border and northern India and gives the impression of a rammed earth style of building construction. In this method, basketlike tubs are used as forms placed along the line of the wall. They are filled with moist dirt, which is then hand-hammered until it is as hard as concrete. The tub is then moved to the next position, and the process is repeated until the wall is complete.

Presenter stand sketch by Alex Wright

These bicycle tracks and footprints in Asia cross over days and days of concrete pours

You're Standing on It

Themed paving is an important aspect of the all-encompassing realism to which Animal Kingdom Park strives. Most of the early paving designs were a fairly straightforward mix of stamped finishes, but the team realized that, for roughly the same cost, they could embed stories into the Park footprint. A series of samples was developed and refined until each one had a place in the Park layout.

These surfaces have to perform all of the functional requirements of normal pavement. They have to hold up to the weather, to constant foot traffic, to parades, to after-hours vehicular traffic, and any unexpected abuse. The team had to develop ways to work in the expansion joints and cold joints that allow the concrete to expand and contract with changes in temperature.

As each texture was being developed, designers studied variations in concrete color, stains, acid washes, and base textures. These textures are captured in silicone stamps or "skins" so that they can be replicated over large areas. Then the team drops in different types of stone or pea gravel to break up those large areas. The team got samples from the landscape architects of the plants that would be found in a given area so that they could use the proper imprint to tie it all together. Elements that help to complete the look for a given place were then rolled across the surface, be they footprints, animal tracks, or bicycle and truck tires. The design team plans a specialized technique for placing expansion joints and cutting cold joints that works for each of the paving styles. Lastly, all of these ingredients are captured into a "recipe" that is documented so that the paving can be replicated when necessary for purposes of maintenance or expansion.

Far Trek

Illustration by Ned Mueller of the Tiger Overlook

Our walking tour of Anandapur takes us far outside the village to the ruins of a former sultan's palace. It has lived a dual life over the years—at one point it was a hunting retreat where painted murals detailed the mastery of Man over the beasts he conquered, currently it is a protected animal sanctuary that shows the effects of the mastery of nature over the works of Man. The walls have been broken down by centuries of exposure to water. There are towers and smaller structures that have been practically disassembled by the force of the trees growing from inside. The aviary was formerly an interior space—a grand ballroom—as indicated by the decorative tiles on the floor and the formal columns in the middle of the room. Through this implication of time and the unstoppable march of Nature to reclaim its superiority over Man, we create a subtext of changing relationships and views toward animals and the natural environment.

Concept by Ned Mueller for the grand ballroom

The history and theme of the attraction are played out right before our eyes through the details left behind over the years. They appear in the murals flanking the entrance and exit of the tiger-viewing rotunda. Four former kings of Anandapur are depicted, each evoking through his stance and his dress different periods in the life of the palace. The first is a hunter, who moves out into the country to build the palace and hunt for game. The next king represents the sensual pleasures, with an urban view toward material wealth. Next is the conqueror who restores the temple after the damage of time and wars. Lastly, the hermit king flees to the forest, hiding from the people and suffering at the whim of nature.

The five-panel bas-relief on the wall near the entrance to the aviary tells the story of the ways in which Man has wrought destruction when he hasn't respected his place in the circle of life—but the final panel indicates that balance can be restored.

Inspirational art of tigers at rest and at play by Nadya Geras-Carson

Tiger Tales

Tigers, for obvious reasons, are one of the featured animals on the Maharajah Jungle Trek. They are seen from three entirely distinct viewing locations, plus a couple of additional bonus views. They demonstrate the power animals hold over us, and the thrill that can be generated by seeing animals in such close proximity to ourselves. This was a key point in the development of the Park. In order to counter concerns that a park about animals might lack some of the excitement of our other parks, Joe Rohde and the Animal Kingdom core team brought a special guest with them to a presentation to Michael Eisner. Unannounced, as Joe delivered his pitch, a tiger was led into the conference room, making one lap of the space before exiting. The question of whether or not animals had the potential to produce great thrills for our Guests was never raised again for the duration of the project!

Bird's-eye illustration of Expedition Everest by Dan Goozee

Reaching New Peaks

The latest addition to Imagineering's mountain range is Expedition Everest—Legend of the Forbidden Mountain. This attraction follows in the grand Disney tradition of breathtakingly ambitious placemaking efforts merged with exhilarating thrill rides—while serving to further the Park's explorations into the idea of mythical animals. The attraction housed in and around this new feature of Animal Kingdom's skyline merges perfectly with all of the central thematic elements that define the Park.

The legend of the Yeti is a common component of the mythologies passed down from generation to generation within many cultures that live in the shadow of the Himalayas. These stories have traveled through Tibet, Nepal, India, and southwestern China, always with certain core elements that are consistent over all those miles and over all these years. These people believe that the Yeti is a real creature, capable of eating a yak from your field when you're not paying attention, but also existing in a mystical realm in which it carries out its protective duties. The Yeti, in their eyes, is a positive force—a protector of the forest—and it is considered a good thing when spotted.

Our attraction takes us to a new place—an extension of our Asia—where we have come to traverse the Forbidden Mountain on our way to Everest. These mountains, however, are a sacred place—and under the watch of the Yeti—so our passage might not be as simple as our tour guides would have us believe. Those old tea trains are in for a bit of a surprise—as are we travelers.

A Solid Foundation—or Three of Them

Any large structure is complicated to build, but Expedition Everest went above and beyond, in more ways than one. The combination of the massive and highly detailed rockwork surface that forms the face of the mountain, the dynamic forces of the high-speed roller coaster, and the immense figure of the Yeti—with his accompanying power—make for one of the most complex construction projects WDI has ever undertaken.

All of the individual systems of the attraction, the building structure, the ride system, and the support for the Audio-Animatronics Yeti are separate and discrete. Each one reaches all the way down to the ground-level foundation without touching any of the other two structures along the way.

All of this complexity was made possible through a piece of 4-D scheduling software developed internally by WDI R & D. This application allows our planners and project managers to see how

Concept for Yeti encounter by Ron Husband

the construction will progress over the course of the build. They are able to visualize via 3-D computer graphics how the site will look at any given time, so that they can avoid conflicts, optimize the delivery of materials, and coordinate various disciplines that need access to the space. Today, WDI uses this tool on all of our big projects.

Concept of tea train embarking on an adventure by Chris Turner

Featured Creature

Early concept of the Yeti by Joe Rohde

Expedition Everest—Legend of the Forbidden Mountain is home to one of the most legendary Audio-Animatronics figures ever created by WDI. It represents our first major foray into the realm of mythical animals, but is housed in one of the most realistic lands of this Park. Our standard in this Park is set by real animals, so the decision was made early on to develop a Yeti that could be believed—if not necessarily compared against any real-world counterpart. Given the devotion to reality of our Forbidden Mountain and the village of Serka Zong, it would not be consistent to plop a silly, cartoony, abominable snowman into the middle of the experience. Our Yeti had to impart an impression on our riders in a very short time and be absolutely convincing in terms of scale, physiology, texture, movement, and sound. Our story is that a legend turns out to be real.

Two concepts by Doug Griffith intended to capture the essence of the figure

Are You Ready, Yeti?

Study model for the Yeti by Doug Griffith

Our Yeti was based on an amalgamation of the various descriptions that have been passed down from generation to generation in the mountains of Tibet, Nepal, India, and southwestern China. These stories were gathered by the design team during their extensive travels in the region.

The team also considered the area of biological research, choosing reference points in the animal world that could combine to form a believable whole. Individual pieces of the skulls of distinct primates were assembled in numerous combinations, offering variations of scale and fit, particularly in the relationship between the upper and lower mandible. There were elements of gibbons, orangutans, and mandrill baboons brought in for reference, but the final combination was primarily that of a langur skull topped off by the sagittal crest of a gorilla. This created unique proportions and attitudes that were then embellished through illustration and even clay modeling directly over the skulls.

Concurrently, the team worked on a critical aspect of any Audio-Animatronics application—the staging and mechanical design. This is where the determination is made how best to place the figure relative to the Guest in order to achieve the desired show—in this case a truly startling and menacing encounter. The Character Concept Designer works to define the number of functions that the figure will require to perform the desired action, then the fabrication team works out the details regarding materials, placement of joints, power supplies, control systems, types of actuators, and structure. These systems are critical, as the Yeti's drive system carries enough hydraulic force to move a passenger jet.

Concept sketch of the fury of the Yeti by Doug Griffith

Kali River Rapids

Bird's-eye view of Kali River Rapids by Ned Mueller

Splashdown

Kali River Rapids takes us on an adventure along the Chakranadi River—Chakranadi being Sanskrit for "river that flows in a circle." This rollicking raft ride through an idyllic mountaintop setting takes a turn we don't expect into an environmental fable about the power of Nature over Man. Our story gets to the root of our constantly evolving attitudes regarding nature and our struggle to achieve harmonic balance. We see the conflicting interests of eco-tourism—the purpose for our trip into the mountain—and unfettered industrialization, typified by the logging company. In our view, the issues presented in Animal Kingdom do not always require resolution, as would be expected in most experiences within our other parks. Our belief is that we've succeeded if we've raised questions and heightened awareness by placing animals and animal issues into these potent situations.

QUICK TAKES

• The souvenirs of Imagineers from the Asia team can be found on one of the paddles on the wall of the booking office in the queue.
• The big drop was mocked up on the grounds of WDI's campus in Glendale for testing of the angle, the distance, and the splash.
• Look for the image of a tiger's face embedded in the rock wall at the top of the lift. It hints at the spirit of the mountain.

The elaborate queue for Kali River Rapids underwent a design process every bit as detailed as that for an attraction. This concept sketch by Ned Mueller hints at the level of detail and placemaking desired by the team. The propping effort for the queue featured over 5,000 individual pieces.

Concept by Zofia Kostyrko for the Asian Safari—a precursor to Kali River Rapids

An Adventure with a Message

As with the rest of the Park, even our grandest adventures are delivered with a conservation message woven into them. Here the issue is that of deforestation. We hear hints of the problems in the distant sounds of chain saws echoing through the queue. There are signs touting the value of the wilderness and warning against deforestation. We begin our travels through this mystical place and are immediately drawn to it.

When the raft enters the burn zone, where a logging company has been unethically stripping the trees off the top of the mountain, we feel a palpable sense of loss. We see the erosion eating away at the banks of the river. We can't understand how people could go into such a magical, inspirational wilderness and do what they've done. The process is so far out of balance that this environment is no longer sustainable. However, in this case, nature has the last word.

The environment is fighting back against this intrusion. The logging truck is teetering on the brink of falling into the rapids because of the erosion of the barren banks. The loggers are not able to continue in their efforts. We are thrown down the great drop and expelled from the area, as we imagine the loggers have been as well.

The burn zone at the top of the mountain is depicted in this concept by Ned Mueller.

Kali River Rapids FastPass distribution structure by Alex Wright

The Story of a Design

As the design for the Kali River Rapids FastPass structure was developed, the team created a story for the place and an identity for the individual who would "live" in this loft. This building is supposed to be located at the edge of our wilderness—the last outpost one encounters before setting out on a trek in search of some natural wonder such as the Chakranadi River. Our FastPass machines are dressed to serve as podiums upon which one might stop to have one's papers reviewed and stamped. The person who mans this station is envisioned as an entrepreneurial sort who has devised every way he can think of to make money from people heading out on such an excursion. We find a bicycle repair stand, a supply of any kind of gear you could need, and provisions of all sorts for sale, to keep you well stocked on the trail.

A High Point in Prop Design

Many pieces among the thousands of props in the queue for Expedition Everest have actually made the climb to the top of the real mountain. Used climbing gear was purchased from outfitters in Nepal.

Tread Marks

The sticks that you see embedded in the "dirt" pathways in many areas of the Park, including Maharajah Jungle Trek, are not really sticks. They're actually concrete castings with a steel rod armature that we fabricate before we pour the path, then place into the wet cement. Real wood would rot away, leaving us with a hole in our walkway.

A Familiar Skyline

On the way in or out of Anandapur, our Everest overlook offers one of the best views of the mountain. In the foreground of this grand vista, you'll see a very special temple that has been built by the villagers. If you study the forms of the temple, you'll see the peaks and masses closely mimicking the mountain range behind it.

Keeping Things in Perspective

Also at the Everest overlook is a map of the range and a telescope that helps Guests spot which of the peaks of the attraction actually represents Mount Everest itself. Tricks of forced perspective—in this case atmospheric effects including desaturation of color and diminishing scale of detail—place the mountain far into the distance.

Don't Miss the Signs

Environmental graphics and signage such as this one found on the bridge from Discovery Island to Asia serve to establish our time and place while embellishing the visual landscape. This sign establishes our location, the date of construction of the bridge, and hints at the existence of a governmental agency responsible for oversight of the town.

DINOLAND, USA

Dinoland, USA is the place where we can have a bit of fun by taking a dig at the animal kingdom. The folks in Dinoland are very happy to see you. Things haven't been the same around here since those fossils were first dug up a few years back, but they wouldn't have it any other way!

Setting the Scene

Bird's-eye illustration of the entrance to Dinoland, USA, by Tom Gilleon

Backstoryosaurus

Dinosaurs may be extinct, but they are still very much a part of the Animal Kingdom story. These amazing creatures are known only through the efforts of humans to learn about them. Our collective ideas about them are shaped by our individual points of view. Dinoland, USA, puts the entire spectrum of attitudes and beliefs about dinosaurs on display for all to see. It bears the imprint of each element of its varied citizenry—ranging from the rigid to the zany.

The original residents of Dinoland predate the discovery of fossils on the site and don't know quite what to make of all the hubbub. Some are just trying (mostly) to go about their business—like the proprietors of Restaurantosaurus—but others have figured out numerous ways to capitalize on the notoriety. Have you seen Chester & Hester's lately?

The most imposing presence in town is that of the Dino Institute, which houses the Dinosaur attraction. The Institute was founded when the mother lode of dinosaur fossils reared its flattened and petrified head. The denizens of this bastion of higher learning are deeply devoted to the science of dinosaurs, and don't have much of a sense of humor about their work. They're stuffy and self-important, and . . . institutional.

But Dinoland really takes its cues these days from the crazy grad students who are enrolled in classes up at the Institute. They leave their mark all over town through pranks and practical jokes. They haven't been reined in by the halls of academia and still see dinosaurs as being fun, fun, fun. Just like we do!

Designosaurus

Like the strata of rock and earth from which we dig up the fossil record, Dinoland reveals its history piece by piece as we dig through layers of design detail. We see the edifice of the massive Dino Institute building and the stodgy and very straightforward signage in the facilities and animal exhibits that they maintain. The staff of the Institute tries to uphold a sense of decorum regarding its paleontological research. They're leery of the crass commercialization of dinosaurs that has taken root since they came to town. They certainly don't condone the more playful activities of the grad students—but they can't control them!

The presence of the irreverent grad students is indicated by the silly tag lines added onto the local signage. The addition of "osaurus" evidently constitutes an improvement to any word. They never miss

an opportunity to tweak their professors and amuse themselves between digs. Note the lawn chairs on the roof of Restaurantosaurus, and the plunger arrows stuck on the side of the adjacent water tower. Also note the handy device they've rigged in order to avoid having to actually exert any effort in retrieving their handiwork.

Of course, Chester & Hester are not to be missed, either. Their quirky style creates an entirely new zone within Dinoland—Chester & Hester's Dino-Rama!—that revels in the exuberant love of dinosaurs. They don't hesitate to have a little fun at the expense of our prehistoric forebears. They can be thanked—or blamed—for all the billboards that clutter the highway attempting to attract some business to their Dinosaur Treasures shop. Chester & Hester will always be there to remind us that there were people here in Dinoland before there were dinosaurs! Well...sort of.

The water tower at Restaurantosaurus shows evidence of a grad-student plunger attack.

The Boneyard

Early concept for The Boneyard by Joe Rohde

Imagineers Reveal Their Inner Children

Playgrounds are fun. They're fun for kids and they're fun for Imagineers. There's nothing better than sitting down in front of a blank sheet of paper, putting yourself into the state of mind of a child, and dreaming up ideas for playtime. Unless you add into that mix the topic of dinosaurs. Now, that's fun!

As a designer, this type of assigment is an excuse to think back to those days when anything and everything could become a plaything. Any object is an opportunity for make-believe. At The Boneyard, we take our setting of a working dinosaur dig site and view it from the point of view of a child. Partially unearthed skeletons become fair game for riding. Any doorway is worth a pull on the handle, just to see who's inside. Any bit of scaffolding or tubing presents a pathway to explore. As we stomp around like dinosaurs—and what kid hasn't?—we make noises that sound as though we're really throwing our weight around.

Paint elevations of rockwork and structures for The Boneyard

Can You Dig It?

We still hold to our mandate for the Park to inform and inspire as we entertain. In The Boneyard, there are numerous opportunities to learn as we play—not least of which is the dig site. Here kids have the chance to uncover a fossil—ours is a combination of bones from a triceratops, a tyrannosaurus rex, and a woolly mammoth, carved by Imagineering sculptors—and learn about how we find the fossils, which leads to our entire body of knowledge

Even a playground doesn't pass on an opportunity to inform as it entertains.

about dinosaurs. Additionally, there are informational plaques scattered around The Boneyard that tell us what paleontologists look for as they dig and study their findings. These graphics make you think about how dinosaurs lived and why they died. If you read closely, you'll see that most of the signs actually showcase a spirited academic debate, with notes posted arguing the printed facts, and championing new theories in the field. That is the true spirit of Dinoland, USA.

Concept illustration by James Wong for The Boneyard

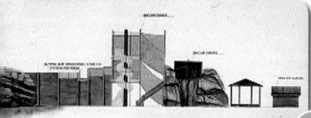

Cretaceous Trail

Happy Trails

These sago palms are examples of cycads.

Sometimes the experiences offered in a Disney park are passive, inviting the Guest to relax, enjoy the scenery, and take in as much or as little as they choose. Cretaceous Trail in Dinoland, USA, is an example of this. It is a sort of botanical garden, maintained by the Dino Institute, that takes one back to a landscape reminiscent of the lands roamed by the dinosaurs millions of years ago.

Being a product of the Institute, the approach here is rather direct. The intent is to inform the visitor, not play around with the subject matter. The dinosaur sculptures we encounter are exceedingly realistic. The content on the graphics located throughout the area is rather straightforward. We're here to learn about dinosaurs and the places they inhabited.

In order to convey this effect, Cretaceous Trail features the third-largest collection of cycads in North America. This collection, gathered by the Park's original landscape design team, consists of plant species that have been around since the age of the dinosaurs. It's a lush, dense environment left mostly devoid of human intervention. In this place, we feel as though we've experienced something of their world.

Sample panels by Gary Graham, Joe Wellborn, Eric Miller, and Colleen Myers

Concrete Examples

At its opening Animal Kingdom represented the absolute state-of-the-art in several of WDI's production disciplines, notably Character Plaster and Character Paint. Owing to the Park's breadth of geography and natural environments, and the unique aging and material qualities that were to be imbued in the surfaces of the architecture, the paint and plaster teams further perfected techniques that raised the bar for this park. Their findings have since been put to use at Tokyo DisneySea and at Disney's California Adventure, among other projects. It makes this park a great place to look at the amazing skills these artists possess.

Character Plaster designers are artists who work with concrete in conjunction with wood, rocks, shells, and other found objects as a medium that they sculpt into the amazing surfaces of our parks. They shape the hardscape, the rockwork, and any building surfaces that go beyond the realm of pure carpentry into replicas of all the various materials we've chosen for our palette. They use tools and implements to cut and press into the surfaces, trowels, and brushes to carve and shape them, and any other substance or device they can think of to impart the essence that will sell the environment to our Guests.

Character Paint art directors actually use much more than *just* paint to do their work. They also apply acid washes, color washes, and stains to achieve the balanced colors we need to see, but often use different techniques before or after that to prepare the surfaces or add just the right touch to the almost-finished piece. For example, the faux moss that we see around many parts of the Park is a mixture of water, glue, and two different colors of painted sawdust thrown at the surface onto which it is to be seen. These processes are very carefully explored and documented during the sample development program and can sometimes involve two dozen steps!

Chester & Hester's Dino-Rama!

Dino-Rama! concept by Chuck Ballew

The Road Less Traveled

Chester & Hester's Dino-Rama! is a mini-land within Dinoland, USA. This amazing assemblage of attractions is the brainchild of our two proprietors. It's a whimsical take on the classic roadside attractions prevalent in the heyday of Route 66. It is intended to be a nostalgic reflection of our appreciation for the intentions of such places, not a cynical view of their creators' somewhat less sophisticated skills as show people. Like many of our fantasy environments, it evokes a place that never really existed in exactly this form, but of which we all somehow carry shared memories. This is a heartfelt place, sincere in its intentions, if not necessarily skilled in its presentations.

In a way that is conceptually similar to Discovery Island, it is an expression of a people's enthusiasm for a subject, and the manner in which they express it. In the case of Dino-Rama!, the subject matter is more specific than in Discovery Island, since all of their attention is focused on dinosaurs, especially on the purely fun side of the topic. There's nothing academic about it. One would imagine that the professors of the Dino Institute don't necessarily frequent this place for their after-hours diversions, but the grad students probably get a kick out of hanging around here when they're done for the day. Still, it seems as though that big Cementosaurus at the entry has attracted enough folks from the highway to stop in for a visit!

Chester & Hester's Dino-Rama! concept featuring TriceraTop Spin by Victor Post

Believe it or not, this faux old, cracked, and sun-blanched asphalt found near Primeval Whirl is one of the most difficult paving styles for the Imagineers to create. Walt learned the hard way on Opening Day at Disneyland that asphalt is not a good choice for a theme park. It softens up in the heat and can grab hold of high heels and other sharp objects. So, we make our "asphalt" out of concrete. The trick is getting the crackle pattern, which involves pouring the right color concrete, embedding a layer of chicken wire just below the surface, and waiting until the concrete is just the right consistency before pulling the wire out. We then carve in all of the big cracks that serve as our joints for expansion and contraction in heat and cold. After that, we sandblast the top so as to expose just the right amount of aggregate for aging.

Primeval Whirl

Vehicle paint elevations by Andrea Bottancino on a design by Jenna Goodman

As We Whirl and Turn

In the world of Chester & Hester, Primeval Whirl makes perfect sense. As little interest as they have in the academic pursuits of the Dino Institute, they're certainly aware of what's going on up there. So, when they found out about the Institute's new Time Rovers, they quickly prepared their response in the competitive marketplace for tourists in Dinoland. However, lacking the ability to actually send anybody back in time, they fall back on their typical approach—cornball comedy!

They devised their own pseudo-time-machine vehicle, put it on a big track with lots of twists and turns, added a bunch of dinosaurs comically approaching their extinction, and then set the whole thing in motion—the only way they knew how. It's a playful, kinetic, frenetic spin on a very important moment in the story of dinosaurs. The end.

Color comps for dinosaur graphic and preshow murals by Andrea Bottancino on designs by Jenna Goodman

TriceraTop Spin concept by Jenna Goodman

Let's Take It for a Spin

One of the most playful elements of Chester and Hester's imaginations is their great big spinning top, the TriceraTop Spin. This evocation of a mid-1950s tin toy dinosaur top is a perfect way to capture the wonder of a child's imagination about dinosaurs. What better way to make a potentially intimidating subject playful and inviting—once a dinosaur has taken you for a ride around the block, what's there to be afraid of?

Vehicle color elevations by Caroline Daley on a design by Jenna Goodman

This marquee graphic designed by Scott Wren captures the classic roadside attraction the way we remember it.

Chester & Hester's Dinosaur Treasures

Every square inch is dinosaurs at Chester & Hester's.

Dino Chic

Chester & Hester's Dinosaur Treasures demonstrates the ability of people everywhere to find some way to make a buck off of anything. Not only are they showing off their own unbounded fascination with dinosaurs, but they're proving our own at the same time! Chester and Hester have taken the opportunity to change over their old-time gas station to a dinosaur gift shop—an attraction in its own right.

This design was a great opportunity for our Prop Designers, as well. The type of set dressing you see around this shop is what the purveyors of this discipline live for. They get to put themselves into the mind-set of a couple of eccentrics like Chester and Hester and see the world through their eyes. This is how we end up with the kind of crazy collection that gives these characters their character. We even get to see the way the world sees them—take a look at the portrait on the wall, in which Chester and Hester bear a *remarkable* resemblance to one another.

It's also a bonanza for our Interior Designers, who go through a similar exercise of trying to understand the residents, but use it as background for the interior finishes and fixtures. They imagine the items that would have been on hand for this renovation, and view them with an eye toward repurposing them in service of the "new" shop. It is through these elements that the Guests come to know Chester and Hester.

QUICK TAKE

• There's a bit of irony built into the fact that a souvenir shop devoted to the exploitation of dinosaurs is located on the site of a former gas station—which exploited dinosaurs in another way, when you think about it.

Restaurantosaurus concept by Topper Helmers

A Building Is Worth a Thousand Words

The Restaurantosaurus building tells the entire story of Dinoland all in one facility—existing as it has since the long-ago days before the first fossil was discovered here. The legend of Dinoland holds that this former fishing lodge sits on the site of that first find—made back in 1947 by an amateur fossil hunter. He and a group of scientist friends banded together to purchase the site, knowing right away how much scientific value would be realized from such a cache. Since its days as a fishing lodge, this building has served as a visitors' center, a museum with fossils on the wall, the first iteration of the Dino Institute with a fossil lab, and a clubhouse for students. Now it's both a commissary and a dormitory for the grad students who live there. They feel a real sense of ownership here, as we see in their handiwork—and displays of their irreverent sense of humor—including the modification of the name on the Restaurant marquee.

All of these lifetimes have left a mark on the building, and each of the rooms carries evidence of its previous function. The Quonset hut is a vehicle maintenance building with an adjacent auxiliary storage. The plastering room has remnants of the prepping and shipping of fossils. The rec room features a basketball hoop—and associated scuffs and dings—along with dartboards, soda cans on the wall, and posters of pop culture items that are of interest to this student crowd. You'll find a variety of awards by and for the students, like the "Zip Award," for the student who works the hardest all summer only to find zip— nothing. Each student has brought a rock from wherever they live and added it to the legacy collection for these "rockhounds."

119

The facade of the Dino Institute

Tree Tops

One of WDI's early happy accidents had a hand in the treatment given to the Dino Institute building. This lesson was learned during the planning of the relocation of "it's a small world" from the site of the 1964-1965 New York World's Fair to Disneyland. As designers in the WED Model Shop tried to figure out how to place this new attraction within the Park, they had left a collection of artificial trees on top of the show building, simply to keep them handy so they could grab them as needed to dress up the attraction's forecourt. One day, they received very short notice that Walt was arriving about thirty minutes early for a review that had originally been scheduled for just after lunch. As he made his way over, the team scurried to dress up the model as well as they could for his inspection. When he walked in, the designers were quickly grabbing the trees and moving them off the building to get them out of the way. Walt said, "Wait," and asked what they were doing. When they answered that the trees were for the forecourt and were just being held there temporarily, Walt told them to stop. He realized right away that trees on top of the building would help to disguise the mass of the building and mask the backstage elements that he didn't want his Guests to see.

This technique was resurrected in the design of the Dino Institute, which needed to be an enormous structure in order to house the Dinosaur attraction. From a story standpoint, however, we didn't want to let on that the building is quite that big. It would be out of place in a sleepy hamlet like Dinoland, USA—giving away the fact that there is a great big attraction waiting for you inside—and would disturb the comfortable pedestrian scale the rest of the land strives to maintain. Sometimes you can't see the show building for the trees!

The Decor's Outdoors

Typically the area outside an attraction or other location will offer a hint of what's in store for you inside. Chester & Hester's is no different. The eclectic mix of ornamentation out front is truly indicative of their...well, unique, sense of...style. The tractor-tire planters suggest a certain creative frugality, and the folk-art dinosaur, sculpted for us by a renowned artist known as Mr. Imagination, demonstrates a whimsical artistic eye. This type of placemaking is a result of Imagineers from multiple disciplines putting themselves creatively into the minds of the local residents.

Weather or Not?

This little shed adjacent to Chester & Hester's, placed there as a shroud for a required utility station, offers a fascinating glimpse into the artistry of our Character Paint group. Even for a seemingly unimportant structure, these designers go to great lengths to develop a backstory that will inform the application of the paint treatment. For example, the team determined the direction of the prevailing wind that would have battered this little shack over the course of its forty or so years of existence. They factored in the protection that would have been offered by the various roof and awning overhangs, and chose not to indicate a history of repainting—as this type of a structure in the world of Chester & Hester's isn't likely to have enjoyed regular maintenance as it would in a Disney park.

Illustration by Joe Rohde of dinosaurs for the eponymous attraction

An Eat-Ticket Attraction

The signature attraction for Dinoland, USA, is Dinosaur, a frenetic chase through prehistoric forests. This adventure takes us back in time to the end of the era of the dinosaurs as Guests encounter the soon-to-be-extinct beasts and attempt to make it back to Animal Kingdom in one piece. The show highlights the tension between the corporate and academic interests of the Dino Institute. This attraction is designed to provide us with a glimpse at a broad range of dinosaur species—from the very docile to the incredibly ferocious—in lifelike Audio-Animatronics form. This Disney-developed art form is the only way you can see these creatures in all their massive, snarling glory—at least until somebody invents a time machine. The veracity of the experience was ensured through consultations with expert paleontologists. The visceral reaction you experience when you find yourself face-to-face with an imposing, absolutely untamed carnotaurus makes a real, educational impact. Besides, it's fun!

Atmospheric concept by Bryan Jowers

EMV Rides Again!

The Enhanced Motion Vehicle ride system used for the Time Rovers in Dinosaur was originally developed for the Indiana Jones™ Adventure at Disneyland, and its advancement was a key component of the tremendous success of that attraction. Dinosaur offers the second-generation design of that vehicle and its first implementation at Walt Disney World. The vehicle consists of a moving platform capable of stopping, going, cornering, climbing, and descending—all while carrying a hydraulic motion base system that offers us the ability to program pitch, roll, and yaw movements to enhance the experience. The real benefit of a vehicle with these capabilities is that it offers us new ways to impart information to the riders. The vehicle can bump as it goes over a log in the trail. It can get bogged down in the mud, or flinch out of fear at a dinosaur attack. It becomes another character in the story.

Storyboards for attack sequences by Christian Hope

QUICK TAKES

•The name of the rogue scientist who bends the rules to send us on our way back to the Cretaceous Period—in another bit of WDI Show Writer wordplay—is Dr. Grant Seeker.

•As you make your way through the load station with the vehicles passing by underneath, pay attention to the white, yellow, and red utility pipes that wind their way throughout the space. The cryptic markings on the sides of the tubes convey the chemical formulas for the very important contents—mayonnaise, mustard, and ketchup!

Dinosaur attack scene illustration by Ben Tripp

"Finding Nemo—The Musical" rendering by Reggie Stanton for Disney Creative Entertainment

Supporting Role

Imagineering is by nature a highly collaborative art, so we greatly enjoy opportunities to work with our partners throughout the company, including those at Disney Creative Entertainment (DCE). In 2006, they debuted a new show for Theater in the Wild called "Finding Nemo—The Musical," carrying on the tradition of animal-related shows in this venue. This inventive production—filled with puppets and lighting effects bringing the undersea world of the Disney•Pixar film to life—even offered up a brand new song so good that we asked DCE's permission to use it in the finale to The Seas with Nemo & Friends at Epcot.

While we can't take credit for what you see onstage, we do play a hand in the presentation of the shows. The creative concepts, the scripts, the set designs, and the overall direction are developed by DCE, but we help out by designing and building the venues in which those shows are performed. "Finding Nemo—The Musical," for example, would not have been possible without the ability to control light offered by the enclosed performance space, added to the facility in 2006.

Theater in the Wild is not really part of any of the lands of Animal Kingdom. Even its name is intended to reflect the idea that it's an entity unto itself. It offers a performance space that can be used for shows that might not fit very well into any of the other established story lines.

Concept elevation of new theater by Alex Wright

I Wanna Play, Too

Kids' Discovery Club at Asia offers animal-spotting tips.

The Kids' Discovery Clubs at Disney's Animal Kingdom are very similar to the Kidcot stations at Epcot. These small-scale adventures put our younger visitors into the role of researcher as they learn about tasks related to conservation or animal care. These opportunities to interact with our Cast Members and ask any questions that may come to mind are incredibly valuable in capturing the imagination of a young explorer.

Each location is dressed to fit in with its land, and the architecture, furniture, and propping further our established story lines. We work with the Park's Education team to find an appropriate activity, then look for a proper means of expressing it within a given land. We design elements such as a crate for a fossil excavation on its way back to the Dino Institute, an outfitter on the fringes of the trekking lands of Asia, and the Camp Counselors' education tents. Kids' Discovery Clubs

Kids' Discovery Club logo by Gary Herpst

allow us to make those story lines relevant to a much younger audience, so that they can feel as though they are part of the action.

At Rafiki's Planet Watch, kids get to spot the makings of successful backyard habitats.

We hope you've enjoyed this tour of Disney's Animal Kingdom as much as we have. Now, you can see the Park through the eyes of an Imagineer. Look for these and so many other little gems hidden in plain sight all throughout the Park. Have fun with the wildlife in this wild place. But most of all, we hope you . . .

Enjoy the Park!

BIBLIOGRAPHY

The Art of Walt Disney, Christopher Finch, Harry N. Abrams, Inc., 1973, rev. 1995, 2004

Building a Dream: The Art of Disney Architecture, Beth Dunlop, Harry N. Abrams, Inc., 1996

Designing Disney: Imagineering and the Art of the Show, John Hench with Peggy Van Pelt, Disney Editions, 2003

Designing Disney's Theme Parks: The Architecture of Reassurance, Karal Ann Marling, Flammarion/CCA, 1997

Disney A to Z: The Official Encyclopedia, Dave Smith, Hyperion, 1996, rev. 1998, 2006

Disney: The First 100 Years, Dave Smith and Steven Clark, Hyperion, 1999, rev. 2002

Disneyland: The Inside Story, Randy Bright, Harry N. Abrams, Inc., 1987

Expedition Everest—Legend of the Forbidden Mountain - The Journey Begins, Jody Revenson, Disney Editions, 2006

Field Guide to Disney's Animal Kingdom Theme Park, Disney Enterprises, Inc., 2000

The Making of Disney's Animal Kingdom Theme Park, Melody Malmberg, Hyperion, 1998

Walt Disney Imagineering: A Behind the Dreams Look at Making the Magic Real, The Imagineers, Hyperion, 1996